"Who better to remind us afresh of what the gospel is than a thoughtful, experienced, post-Christendom evangelist like John Bowen? He has the gift of discussing the complex, dynamic intersection of gospel, church, and culture in understandable, easy-to-listen-to ways. This is a much-needed, back-to-basics book that helps God's people reaffirm the goodness of the good news."

—AL TIZON, affiliate associate professor of missional and global leadership, North Park Theological Seminary, and executive minister of Serve Globally Evangelical Covenant Church

"Once again, John Bowen excels here in communicating with convincing clarity, warmth, grace, and faithfulness about the blessings that abound in sharing and living out the gospel in the world God loves. Laypeople, church leaders, and anyone interested in 'what's next' for the church and the Christian movement will find this an engaging and worthwhile read."

—ROB FENNELL, academic dean, Atlantic School of Theology, and author of *The Rule of Faith and Biblical Interpretation: Reform, Resistance, and Renewal*

"John Bowen writes as if you were having a conversation at the kitchen table over coffee, responding to unasked questions while exploring the great themes of the gospel, with stories from his experience as a teacher and theologian that capture the heart and imagination. With a thorough knowledge of Scripture, church history, and C. S. Lewis, alongside his experience mentoring evangelists and church planters, he invites us to hold firmly to the core of the gospel and lightly to what may need to change. He does it all with the joy and passion of his own winsome evangelistic gifts. A book for all grappling with the future of the church!"

—ARCHBISHOP LINDA NICHOLLS, primate, Anglican Church of Canada

"With his usual wit and wisdom, John Bowen continues his lifelong commitment to equipping scholarly evangelists for church and academy in *The Unfolding Gospel*. Bowen is a docent for the reader in both senses of the word. First, his university classroom experience is evident in this thoughtful and theological exploration of evangelism. Second, he is a docent in the sense that he serves as a cheerful guide moving the reader through the 'gospel gallery,' reinterpreting everything from conversion to church planting along the way. *The Unfolding Gospel* is a must read for those curious about how to live, share, and speak the gospel as a faithful witness to God's redeeming presence in the world today."

—ROSS LOCKHART, dean of St. Andrew's Hall,
Vancouver, and author of *Lessons from Laodicea:
Missional Leadership in a Culture of Affluence*

"In *The Unfolding Gospel*, John Bowen brings his gentle humor and his perceptive observations to the business of telling the gospel story. If, like me, you sometimes feel that the gospel is 'otherworldly' or that 'evangelism' is best left to the extroverted or a special class of Christian, then this book will restore your confidence. Reading this book reminds you that Jesus journeys with us right where we are and that the gospel is always for these times and places."

—BETH GREEN, provost of Tyndale University,
Toronto, and regional editor of the *International
Journal of Christianity and Education*

"Encountering John Bowen in print is not unlike encountering him in the flesh: wise, passionate, and articulate with an occasional dash of welcome irreverence! Each of these is abundantly evident in his fulsome exploration of how the good news has become—and is becoming—alive in discipleship, church, mission, and everything else! You will enjoy this engaging conversation with a trusted friend who knows how to both provoke and inspire."

—MICHAEL J. PRYSE, bishop, Eastern Synod,
Evangelical Lutheran Church in Canada

"Finally! A book for those who want to follow Jesus and are serious about inviting others to do the same. John Bowen's background in the English Renewal Movement, his participation in all things missional in North America, and his commitment to scholarliness make this an outstanding book. He not only lives this out but has helped many others like me learn to walk in the way of Jesus also. Now this book, written in his usual winsome and wonderful manner, will help many, many more live out the good news of the kingdom of God. I can't wait to get my hands on multiple copies to give away."

—CAM ROXBURGH, global director of Forge Missional
Network; team leader of Southside Community Church,
Vancouver; and contributor to *Green Shoots out of Dry
Ground: Growing a New Future for the Church in Canada*

"*The Unfolding Gospel* is an essential gospel primer for pastors, church planters, and regular run-of-the-mill apprentices of Jesus—the fruit of decades of teaching, practice, and thoughtful and prayerful reflection. John Bowen is a wise guide: logical, engaging, witty, honest, and sure footed as he leads us forward into the post-Christendom and postpandemic landscape."

—JILL WEBER, member of the international leadership
team of 24-7 Prayer; director of Spiritual Formation
at Emmaus Road Church, Guildford, United Kingdom;
and author of *Even the Sparrow: A Pilgrim's Guide
to Prayer, Trust, and Following the Leader*

"What John Bowen has masterfully accomplished in this book is a bird's-eye view of the interconnectedness of many areas in our lives and how they all are linked to the sharing of the good news of Jesus Christ. Though he is a man of deep wisdom and theological knowledge who cares deeply for the good news, he imparts this with equally deep humility and humor."

—PILAR GATEMAN, executive officer and archdeacon
of Calgary in the Anglican Diocese of Calgary

The Unfolding GOSPEL

The Unfolding GOSPEL

How the **Good News** *Makes Sense of* **Discipleship, Church, Mission,** *and* **Everything Else**

[handwritten: For Joan ~ with all good wishes! John Bowen May 1st 2022]

John P. Bowen
Foreword by David Fitch

FORTRESS PRESS

MINNEAPOLIS

THE UNFOLDING GOSPEL
How the Good News Makes Sense of Discipleship, Church, Mission, and
Everything Else

Print ISBN: 978-1-5064-7167-9
eBook ISBN: 978-1-5064-7168-6

Cover design: Marti Naughton / sMartdesigN
Cover images: ID: 186827634 © petekaric | iStock

To the Hamilton Pioneer Cohorts:

*"Every time you cross my mind, I break out
in exclamations of thanks to God."*

Philippians 1:3 MSG

CONTENTS

FOREWORD

Christians today are bewildered in the midst of the cultural changes taking place in North America. In the span of just one lifetime, many Christians have moved from being in the majority of the culture to being a minority that is often viewed with suspicion, and even resentment, by the people around them. Where Christianity once dominated the culture, Christians now live in a society of multiple cultures where no one religion is the majority faith. The swiftness of these changes is dizzying. The magnitude of these changes is overwhelming.

The elder Christians among us remember a time when the church held a position of respect and influence in most North American cities and towns. Pastors and clergy were welcomed regularly into the schools or chambers of government. They were sought after for their advice and approval. Society as a whole, it seemed, would look to the church for moral guidance. Today that is all but gone. Who today dares bring a Bible with them to a local public school meeting? Even the language of Christians no longer connects with the culture. Christian words like *sin* and *salvation* now need to be explained when we use them outside the walls of a church building. When we say "God," people ask, "Which one?" What are we to make of the future of the church that is now cast into such a sea of unfamiliarity?

When culture changes this fast and the rug gets pulled out from beneath our feet, we should expect knee-jerk reactions. The church has often reacted in knee-jerk fashion to these changes by either getting defensive or trying to accommodate. When the church gets defensive, it gets confrontational with those who challenge what it believes. It tries to hold on to lost authority and works urgently to preserve its way of life among a smaller and shrinking group of people. In the end, a defensive church retreats and fails to engage the ills or confusions of its surrounding culture. On the other hand, when the church gets accommodative, it tries quickly to become relevant to the changes, hoping to preserve its stake in influencing the culture. It tries to agree as much as possible with the existing culture in the hope of making friends and influencing people. This approach, instead of engaging cultural issues, blends in with the culture. Although both the defensive and the accommodative reactions are understandable, neither really engages the struggles, ills, and pains of its culture.

Ultimately, these defensive and accommodative reactions are power moves from a time when the church had cultural authority. Back then, it would defend its beliefs and people would listen. Back then, it had influence in the culture, so it expected to be relevant. When you're used to being in charge, defending yourself or using your cultural influence is what you do. Old habits die hard. But the passing away of the Christendom culture has made both of these approaches to engage the culture either presumptive or offputting. The church is badly in need of another option.

In what follows, John Bowen offers us another option. He starts with the only thing the church can offer to a world in massive cultural flux: the gospel. There is no defensiveness or accommodation to his approach. Instead, he begins with a careful clarification of what the gospel is. For John, the "big statement" of the gospel is "the good news of what God is like, that God the Creator is on a mission to right all wrongs through Jesus Christ." He unfurls what this gospel entails for human life in all its true glory and then allows this gospel to unwind all our assumptions about what we are doing that we call church. John allows the gospel to do the work of realigning what we do as a church as we engage culture. After John is done, the church cannot help but become a full participant in the mission of God in the culture, because it is living out the gospel.

Please do not mistake John's option for an oversimplistic proposal that the gospel is all we need. He's not saying that simply preaching the gospel will meet the challenges we face in being Christians in the secularized West. John is doing so much more than that. He is leading us through the church's mounting problems, its massive disconnect with culture, and its hangover of bad habits from Christendom that many of us have experienced as Christians these past few decades. He helps us understand them all through a clarifying of the gospel.

With remarkable candor, John untangles the dilemmas, unwinds the assumptions, and attacks the frameworks, which then opens pathways for the gospel to realign all we do as churches. Everything we do as a church, including worship, evangelism, discipleship, and church planting, gets illumined by the gospel. After reading each chapter, working through each issue of being church, we have a sense of what we can discard and what is essential to retain in being the church. He does not throw away the great traditions of our faith. Instead, he carefully discerns their purpose and refashions them through the lens of the gospel. Through it all, what John is doing is giving us an alternative to the defensiveness and accommodation of our age as we engage our changing culture. It is the option of a new faithfulness for mission.

So I encourage the reader to sit back, take a deep breath, and allow what follows to impact your soul. Let this book challenge your mind and reshape your vision for what is possible in the Christian life. Let John Bowen shape in us all a new faithfulness for mission, one the church desperately needs in the secular West.

David Fitch
Betty R. Lindner Chair of Evangelical Theology
Northern Seminary, Lisle, Illinois

INTRODUCTION
(The Kind You Really Need to Read)

This is a superficial book, and I feel good about that. In my opinion, there are far too many deep books around, and it is time someone provided an alternative.

Superficial? I bought my granddaughter a globe for Christmas. Not any old globe, however. This one came in the form of a four-hundred-piece three-dimensional jigsaw puzzle. Yes, really. If you started at the bottom, with the South Pole, the pieces could be put together one after another, in a kind of spiral, until you reached the North Pole—and there you had the world. Very cool.

But it was a superficial gift, in the same way that this is a superficial book. Abby could learn all sorts of stuff about individual countries, or even individual continents, and do so in great depth. But to stand back and see the world as a whole puts everything into perspective. The depth and the superficiality are both necessary for a full understanding.

This book covers a wide waterfront: huge topics like gospel, mission, discipleship, church, evangelism, culture, leadership, and so on. Inevitably, I only touch on each one quite briefly, and I suspect you will find this frustrating at times. (Did I mention the book was superficial?)

But this skimming of the surface is intentional. My goal is not to explore these topics in depth, because others have done that, and continue to do that, far better than I could do. What I am trying to do—and I don't think this is so often done—is to try to show the connection among all these things. And that, I like to believe, has the same kind of value as having a globe of the world.

OTHER THINGS YOU NEED TO KNOW

We are all culturally situated. We were born at a particular time in a particular place. We have all been shaped by whatever influences our families of origin brought to bear on us and by whatever was going on in the culture and the wider world around us. That's just the way it is. We can't escape that reality, and (as I argue in chapter 7) it is a good thing, and a God-given thing.

But it does help if we are aware of what has shaped us and realize that those things are not absolutes. For one thing, to be self-aware about these influences, and to be upfront about them, nurtures humility in us. We tend to be less dogmatic. We are more likely to say "I could be wrong, but . . ." or "I realize I may be a bit biased in saying this, but . . ." This is a particularly important posture when we are talking to people who have been shaped differently (date of birth, place of origin, parental influences, cultural forces, and so on)—which is more or less everyone on the planet— and trying to communicate across those divides.

So it will help as you read this book to know some of the things that have shaped me. I hope that will help you make allowances. It will mean you can sit lightly to some of the things I say ("Well, naturally, he would think that . . .") while taking others more seriously ("Hmm, that's a different perspective: I'll have to think about that").

WHERE I AM COMING FROM

I was born in 1946, just after the Second World War, so yes, I am an early baby boomer. My parents were born just after the First World War, so they grew up between those wars, and that was part of what shaped them. I am white, middle class (my father was an architect, and my mother never worked outside the home), and privileged (I spent four years at Oxford University). Even during the lean times in the early years of our marriage, when we sold possessions to have enough to live on, I never doubted that we would have food on the table and a roof over our heads. I hope I am duly thankful.

I have a strong sense of roots. I was born in Wales, not England, and three of my family of four voted for the Welsh Nationalist Party, Plaid Cymru. (I don't think it's betraying confidences at this stage to say that my mother was the odd one out.) I grew up in the house my grandparents had bought when they married in 1904 and in which my father had been born.

From my early years, I was made aware that the Welsh had been oppressed and colonized by the English for seven hundred years and that we had survived. But I recognize now that on the whole, we had survived largely by assimilation. One example will illustrate. My father grew up speaking the Welsh language at home, but by the time he married my mother (who was English), he spoke Welsh only in conversation with his mother, who lived with us, and with certain clients who preferred Welsh. I learned Welsh in high school for a few years but never became fluent. You would never know I was Welsh from my accent or from anything else except the Welsh flag on my bumper, unless I told you. But that sense of being Welsh, and therefore distinct and outsider-ish, goes very deep. Hence the bumper sticker.

SPIRITUAL ROOTS

Spiritually, I grew up in my mother's church, which was Anglican, a denomination that came from England and never managed to put down deep roots in Welsh soil. As a teenager, I was deeply impacted by a religious education teacher in high school. (In those days in the UK, religion was a required subject, and "religion" meant Christianity.)

That brought me into an evangelical form of Christianity that in one way or another has nurtured me ever since. It grew and evolved through university (with involvement in InterVarsity Christian Fellowship [IVCF], where I met my wife), seminary (Trinity College, Bristol), work for IVCF (in the UK from 1973 until 1977 and then in Canada until the late 1990s), and my last paid job, as professor of evangelism at Wycliffe College in the University of Toronto (1997–2016).

I like to qualify the much-despised term *evangelical* by saying I am an Anglican evangelical, which I realize sounds to some like an oxymoron. In the early years of my spiritual formation, I turned my back on the Anglican church in which I had grown up and favored Baptist and Congregational churches instead. But at university, I encountered churches and teachers who were happy to identify as Anglican and evangelical, and I immediately felt at home. The evangelical fire seemed to burn brightly in the Anglican fireplace.

I should add that this background has not stopped me from learning from and being enriched by other Christian traditions: Catholic and Orthodox, Reformed, Charismatic, and Anabaptist. Some of those influences will become obvious.

Like most evangelicals (but not only evangelicals[1]) these days, I have been deeply influenced by C. S. Lewis, which in a way is strange because Lewis would not have self-identified as an evangelical. He describes himself as "a very ordinary layman of the Church of England, not especially 'high,' nor especially 'low,' nor especially anything else"—in other words, as a "mere Christian."[2] In his day, the evangelical movement was probably narrower and more partisan than it is now, which may explain why he did not associate with it.[3]

Lewis has become the single biggest influence on my understanding of Christianity, as will be obvious from the many references and notes. I think I particularly appreciate that, like me, he was not ordained (and would have been horrified at the suggestion). His theology was self-taught and incredibly far-ranging. I remember checking one of his quotations (unfootnoted) and found it was deeply buried within the third volume of Thomas Cranmer's collected works. That's typical. I love too the way he models thoughtful, intellectually responsible evangelism. Because he was a layperson involved in the secular world all of his life, the questions he tackles are usually the ones ordinary people ask, not the ones religious professionals (like me) think people ask, or should ask.

My other influences, some of whom will be apparent, include, in my teens and twenties, John Stott, Michael Green, David Watson, and Alec Motyer; later, from the end of the last century, Lesslie Newbigin, Vincent Donovan, David Bosch, Andrew Walls, and Lamin Sanneh; and more recently, Tom Wright, Christopher Wright, George Sumner, Brian Walsh, Jamie Smith, Andy Crouch, and David Fitch.

And before you point it out, yes, I am painfully aware that all but one of these are white males from the Global North. I can only say, if I were beginning my career now, it would be different. For the record, I am presently working my way through *Walking the Good Road*, the First Nations Version of the Gospels, and Fleming Rutledge's magisterial *The Crucifixion: Understanding the Death of Jesus Christ*.[4]

Also, on the personal side, if you care about personality types, Myers-Briggs would say that I am an INFJ. (I was an INTJ for many years but have become more F since retiring from academia. Go figure.) And on the Enneagram, I am a clear Five—the Observer. We like being outsiders. We enjoy making sense of things in our heads. Just don't bother us with that messy thing—what is it you call it?—oh yes, "reality." Fives often turn into teachers. My propensity to observe, to want to make sense of things, and to teach is pretty clear in what follows. Maybe also my impatience with "reality."

WHAT I AM (AND AM NOT) DOING HERE

Today, there is an ongoing conversation about the future of the church and "the turn to the missional," beginning with the writings of Lesslie Newbigin and continuing after his death in 1998, in the work of people like George Hunsberger, Craig Van Gelder, David Fitch, Alan Hirsch, Alan Roxburgh, and many others.

It is an important conversation because it involves the future of the Christian movement, particularly in the West, addressing such fundamental questions as, What is the church? and What is its mission? The conversation needs to continue, but I need to say at the outset, I am not trying to contribute directly to it or move it forward. For those on the cutting edge, much of what follows will be familiar territory, even "old hat." But the cutting edge of the knife needs a handle that is firm and reliable. Maybe I can strengthen the handle and thus make the cutting edge more precise.

What I am hoping is that, rather than advancing the conversation, I may reach an audience of people just beginning to think about the future of the church and the meaning of the word *missional* and bring them up to speed by filling in the background and context against which the conversation is happening.

In particular, I am writing for people who are new to the whole topic of missional church, hence my attempt to begin at the beginning. I have in mind such groups as first-year seminary students; older people in whose lifetime church has changed drastically and who are trying to understand what has happened and whether there is a way forward; their pastors, who are trying to find ways to teach and encourage those older congregations; and young people who are involved in lively church plants but who have maybe not yet reflected on why their churches are doing what they are doing. I have presented different parts of these materials to all of these groups in recent years and seem to have connected with all. Whether it works in your context, you will have to judge.

THE ORIGINS OF THIS BOOK

In 2002, Augsburg Fortress published my first book, *Evangelism for "Normal" People*. I have been gratified to find over the intervening years that church groups have studied it, and it has been a textbook in several seminaries of different denominations.

Then two things happened. In 2014, my friend Andy Rowell, now assistant professor of ministry leadership at Bethel Seminary in Saint Paul, Minnesota, contacted me. He was using *Evangelism for "Normal" People* as a textbook in an evangelism class and wondered if I would be willing to Skype with the class at the end of the semester. How could I say no? But having said yes, I thought, "Hmmm, I haven't picked that book up for a long time. What exactly did I say in there?" I suspect it is generally true that authors don't often reread their books once they're published, and I am no exception.

Well, reading it was a revelation. Sure, there were a lot of things that I would still say now. In fact, you will come across lots of notes referring to "Normal" People, where it supplements what I am writing here.

But in almost two decades of teaching, interacting with churches, and being involved in ministry since that book came out, my understanding had evolved. At first, I thought I could simply revise "Normal" People. I tried, and it was one of the most frustrating exercises I have undertaken. Didn't someone once say something about new wine and old wineskins?

What was the problem? There were several points where the wine didn't fit into the wineskin. The following are some examples:

- In "Normal" People, "What Is the Gospel?" doesn't appear until chapter 10. Now I have made it chapter 1 because I have come to the conviction that everything depends on that starting point.

- There is little about discipleship in "Normal" People. Yet there is no clear explanation of the gospel that does not imply a theology of discipleship and a call to follow Jesus. If, as you sometimes hear, people have "accepted Jesus as their savior but not as Lord," I frankly believe that the explanation of the gospel they heard was deficient. So discipleship now plays a part—another two chapters—in this new book.

- It is pretty clear now that more people come to Christian faith in new churches than in older ones. When I realized this, I introduced a course on church planting (which I continue to teach) at Wycliffe College and added a chapter on the subject to this book.[5]

The first book more or less worked its way through the Bible from Genesis to Revelation. There is a logic to the sequence in this book too, but here the progression is more theological, as will quickly become clear. I think both approaches work well, but in a sense, this one provides a wider context for the first. I think of it this way. My son is taller than I am, and his teenage daughter looks set to grow taller than he is. I have photos with my father, and of him with his father, and this trend has clearly been going on since the 1930s. So with these two books: the second has the DNA of the first, but this one (to my mind, anyway) has somehow grown taller; it's the next generation.

WHAT'S HERE—AND WHAT ISN'T

The book begins with a consideration of what we mean by "the gospel." To my mind, this is the key to everything else, as I will explain. Once we grasp that, a lot of other things fall into place—words that are easily tossed around and given different meanings, like *mission*, *discipleship*, and *evangelism*. Once the gospel is at the heart of the jigsaw puzzle, the other pieces fall into place around it. I then try to trace how the gospel informs—or should inform—our understanding of such things as mission, church, culture, and leadership.

Kind friends have suggested chapters I might add—on social justice, on the environment, on Sabbath, on culture making, on forms of training for ministry, or on the arts—and that's just for a start. But those are beyond my very limited expertise—even though I do think that in principle the gospel speaks to each of those areas. Just as God made all of life, just as sin has touched every aspect of that life, so Christ's good news works to redeem the whole of life. As C. S. Lewis says, "There is no neutral ground in the universe: every square inch, every split second, is claimed by God and counter-claimed by Satan."[6] If I can address even one of those square inches, I will be content.

CHAPTER 1

WHAT IS THE GOSPEL?
Complexity and Simplicity

When Winston Churchill was prime minister of Britain, he was once told that the leader of the opposition party was a very humble man. "Well," said Churchill, "he has a lot to be humble about." In my years as a professor of evangelism, one of the (many) things that kept me humble was the knowledge that in the early centuries of the Christian movement, it grew faster than almost any comparable movement in human history.[1] Yet the first Christians had no training in evangelism, no books on evangelism, and certainly no help from professors of evangelism. So how did they do it? Let's come at this indirectly.

Howard Schultz, the former CEO (now executive chairman) of Starbucks, has apparently said that he wants every Starbucks customer to become "a Starbucks evangelist." The meaning is obvious, isn't it? He wants everyone who visits a Starbucks to be so excited about the experience that they can't help talking to their friends about it: "Do you know what Starbucks is offering this week? It is amazing! You absolutely have to go and check it out."

There is an assumption that if the experience is powerful enough and delightful enough, people will spontaneously talk about it with their friends. The best (and certainly the shortest) definition of evangelism I ever heard was "Evangelism is overflow."[2] That's what Starbucks is aiming at: an overflow of enthusiasm about what they have to offer.

There are no books you need to read in order to be a Starbucks evangelist, no training courses to attend, no pithy quotes from Howard Schultz for you to memorize. All you need is a great experience at Starbucks, and the rest will follow—the less scripted the better.

Something of this kind was at play in the growth of Christianity. But what was it that those early Christians were enthusiastic about? It wasn't Starbucks or even coffee, so what was it that overflowed to the world around and drew others to this new movement?

You can learn a lot from what people talk about and how often they talk about it. (Have I mentioned my grandchildren yet?) Thus I can't help noticing that the words the New Testament uses most frequently when discussing Christian faith are significantly different from the words we use in churches today. Let me show you what I mean.

There is a simple, even simplistic, kind of Bible study I call "statistical theology." Many forms of theology are very complicated, but anybody who can count to a hundred can do this kind. It works like this: How many times is a certain word used in a particular book of the Bible or in the Bible as a whole? This approach doesn't prove anything conclusive, of course, but it can provoke productive reflection.

Here's something I noticed. Think about some of the words you hear most frequently in church life, and then compare that with the number of times they are used in the New Testament. When I did this, I found something very surprising. Here's a list:

TOPICS WE TALK ABOUT	NUMBER OF TIMES IN NEW TESTAMENT
Fellowship	7
Ministry	22
Pray/prayer	25
Forgiveness	36
Money	37
Worship	53
Preaching	56
Church	76

If you are familiar with the life of a local congregation, I suspect you would agree that these are some of the words you hear most often in discussing the church's life. (It is true that I haven't included the words *committee*, *organ*, or *budget*. Maybe I just missed them.)

But there is one word that is used more frequently than any of those: that word is *gospel*. How often is that word used in the New Testament? Over a hundred times![3] In other words, it occurs more often than the words *fellowship*, *ministry*, *prayer*, and even *forgiveness*—combined.

So here is the question that comes to my mind: Could it be that the early growth of the church was somehow connected to this thing called the gospel? And might the decline in the church in the West be connected with the fact that we don't talk about the gospel much? I did some field research to try to find out.

GOSPEL? WHAT GOSPEL?

One experience came when I was leading a workshop on evangelism and said something about "the gospel." An elderly gentleman in the front row spoke up and said, "I've been in church all of my life, and I can't say I have ever heard anything I would call 'the gospel.'" Unfortunately (or perhaps fortunately), his minister was sitting beside him, and he turned to him open-mouthed: "But you hear it every Sunday!" he gasped.

So who was right? In a way, both of them were. If I were cynical (and it may shock you to know that I can be), I would guess that the minister meant, "Every Sunday you hear a reading from one of the four New Testament Gospels." That would have been true. Or, if I were more charitable (and I can be), the minister may have meant that the gospel, the good news, is woven into everything in the service—the readings, the hymns, the prayers, certainly the sermon (I'm not sure about the announcements)—so how can you not have heard it? If that's what the minister meant, then yes, that church member had "heard" the gospel. But *gospel* means "good news"—and somehow that gentleman had never heard anything in his seventy-something years in church that struck him as really, really good news. There had been no Sunday when his eyes lit up and he said, "So *that's* why they call it good news!"[4] Very sad, but I have heard that kind of story often enough to know that it is not uncommon.

The Gospel of Loving Your Neighbor

In another group, I again asked the question "What is the gospel?" This time another lifelong churchgoer replied, "The gospel? That's easy. Love your neighbor as yourself." To which my answer was, "If you knew me, and you knew my neighbors, you would know there is no good news in that." Don't get me wrong. I really like my neighbors—I couldn't ask for better—and from time to time, I will happily do something nice for them. (Feed the cat and take in the mail while you're away? Sure.) But love them *as much as I love myself*? Dream on. That's way beyond me. There's no good news in that—not for me and certainly not for my neighbor.

In the New Testament, whatever the gospel is (and we will get there), it is never something I have to do, never a burden or a responsibility laid on me. (Thanks be to God for that.) Certainly, once I understand and begin to experience the gospel, this new life entails certain responsibilities, but it doesn't begin there. Never. At its heart, "Christianity is a rescue religion," says John Stott.[5] It is primarily about God doing for me something that I cannot do for myself. In fact, more recently, when I have asked people to state the gospel, I have specified, "Make it a sentence beginning with the word *God*." You would be surprised how often people can't do it.

The Gospel According to John 3:16

Another common answer to the question "What is the gospel?" is John 3:16: "God so loved the world that he gave his only Son, so that everyone who believes in him may not perish but may have eternal life." Well, yes, it is a wonderful verse. In fact, I have always felt slightly embarrassed that I was helped to a personal faith by

John 3:14. It seemed wrong somehow—as if I had just missed the bull's-eye that everybody else had managed to hit.

I do notice, however, that John never uses the word *gospel* in what we like to call "The Gospel of John." Neither does he give any indication that he (or indeed Jesus) thought this verse was special. It's just there in the middle of a long speech, with no neon flashing lights around it to draw attention to it. It's an interesting historical question when and why this verse was singled out as the definitive statement of "the gospel."[6] But there is absolutely no reason to think we should take it that way.

The Gospel According to the Apostle Paul

What about the apostle Paul? After all, his letters precede the writing of the gospels and so give us a window into life in the earliest years of the church.[7] There are three places in his writings where he appears to give us a definition of "the gospel," which you would think might help. However, it's confusing, since they differ quite considerably. Let's look at them.

In Romans 1:1–4, Paul writes about "the gospel of God, which he promised beforehand through his prophets in the holy scriptures, the gospel concerning his Son, who was descended from David according to the flesh and was declared to be Son of God with power according to the spirit of holiness by resurrection from the dead, Jesus Christ our Lord."

To be perfectly honest, I don't know any evangelist who preaches the gospel this way. "Hey, did you know Jesus is descended from King David? Isn't that amazing?" No: if that is really good news, we will need to understand a little more than that. Quite apart from that, the whole statement is a bit odd, since there is resurrection but no crucifixion (Isn't that pretty important? How can you have one without the other?), no talk of atonement and forgiveness, no mention of reconciliation with God. Surely that can't be the whole of what Paul means by good news?

Here's the second statement by Paul: the gospel is "that Christ died for our sins in accordance with the scriptures, and that he was buried, and that he was raised on the third day in accordance with the scriptures" (1 Cor 15:3–4). This seems closer to what we generally think of as the gospel: that through the death of Christ our sins are forgiven and that Jesus has risen from the dead.

It's true that both these statements of Paul's focus on Christ, both mention resurrection, and both refer to the biblical witness to Christ. But one stresses forgiveness, which the other doesn't. One stresses Jesus's royal descent, which the other doesn't.

Let's mix things up a little more. If we go back to John 3:16, that statement of the gospel sounds very different from either of those definitions of Paul's. John talks about God's love, about believing, and about eternal life—things Paul doesn't even mention—while John leaves out things that Paul seems to have considered crucial, such as the death of Christ, the resurrection, the atonement, and Jesus's royal descent.

Let me throw in the third example. In Galatians (3:8), Paul says, "The scripture, foreseeing that God would justify the Gentiles by faith, declared the gospel beforehand to Abraham, saying, 'All the Gentiles shall be blessed in you.'"[8] This is a reference to Genesis 12:2–3. Now, I have often asked people what they think the gospel is, and I have heard many different answers. However, I've never yet had anyone say, "Well, clearly the gospel is Genesis 12:2–3. Isn't it obvious?" So what on earth is going on here? The gospel is words spoken by God to Abraham over a thousand years before Jesus came? How is this possible?

Are you confused yet? Now, this question of what the gospel is could just be one of those areas where we say, "Well, you know what? The Bible isn't clear about this, so let's not worry about it." However, we really can't do that for this topic. Apart from anything else, according to Paul, the gospel is not just a neat idea: the gospel is a gift from God entrusted to the church—a miracle drug for the human affliction, if you like—and to dilute it by taking away from it or to adulterate it by adding to it is more or less criminal. Paul actually says that if you do that, you are "accursed" by God (Gal 1:8–9)—the kind of language we are rather too polite to use. But that's how Paul saw it.

So if the issue is so important, why this confusion? Why does Paul appear to contradict himself? And why don't he and John say the same things? Clearly, we haven't gotten to the heart of this yet.[9] If these explanations of "the gospel" are inadequate and confusing, where can we begin?

The Gospel According to You

Another approach I have tried is to ask people what "the gospel" means to them. I have already suggested that in one sense, the gospel is always expressed best in a sentence beginning with the word God. But in this exercise, I actually encourage people to begin their sentence with the word I. I am probing the personal impact of this thing that God has done. And the answers I get are far-ranging and often touching:

- I know I am loved by God.
- I have a place in God's family.
- I find my life has been turned outward.
- I am a child of God.
- I face each day with hope.
- I am not the person I once was.
- I find that all the different aspects of my personality come together in my relationship with God.
- I have a friend in Jesus.
- My life has meaning from following Jesus.
  (I decided to allow my instead of I in this case.)

In one group of Presbyterians where we did this exercise, after several such contributions, one man stood up and said loudly, "I think we should stand and sing 'Praise God from whom all blessings flow'!" Which we promptly did. I told them I had never before thought of Presbyterians as given to spontaneous outbursts of praise, but the gospel does funny things to people.

Of course, there is a downside to this approach: if we are trying to establish a core meaning for "the gospel," all these answers are very different.

BRINGING IT ALL TOGETHER

Here's an analogy I find helpful. I was born just after the Second World War. After the end of that war in 1945, many things changed, especially in Britain. There was lots of good news. The danger of Nazism was ended, and democracy appeared to be safe. People came home from the armed forces, got married and had children, and some went to university. Children who had been sent away to the country to avoid the bombing in the cities were able to go back home.[10] Thick curtains that had to be put over windows at night to keep any light from escaping were folded away forever. Food rationing came to an end. And street signs, which had been taken down to confuse any possible invaders, were put back.

So the good news took many forms. One might say, "My husband came home"; another might say, "The government paid for me to go to university"; and a child might say, "I got to eat bananas for the first time." And there is no obvious way those three things could be connected—unless you knew the big overarching truth that these were all trickle-down effects of the one huge thing that had happened: the war had ended.

What if all those varied statements of "the gospel" that we have listed were like that? They are all true for someone, obviously, but none of them is the full truth. If you like, those too are the trickle-down effects of one big overarching truth, the equivalent of saying, "The war is over." (See figure 1.1.)

So the million-dollar question is, What is that big statement of good news?

THE GOSPEL ACCORDING TO JESUS

Maybe it's time we asked what Jesus said about this subject of the gospel. Mark's Gospel opens by saying it is "the beginning of the good

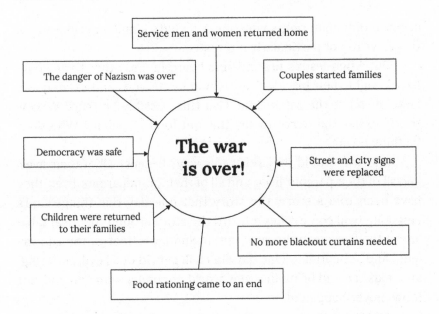

FIGURE 1.1. The war is over

news of Jesus Christ, the Son of God" (Mark 1:1), so that's an encouraging start. And shortly afterward, when Jesus makes his first public statement, that too is about the gospel: "The time is fulfilled, and the kingdom of God has come near; repent, and believe in the good news" (Mark 1:15).

I used to think, when I read the words "believe in the good news," "So Jesus, when exactly are you going to tell us the gospel? Don't keep us hanging like this!" But now I realize, of course, the gospel is not something he's *going* to say; it's something he has just said: the kingdom is at hand! That is Jesus's gospel in a word: the kingdom.

We don't get terribly excited about this idea of the kingdom, do we? It's probably because "kingdom" means something rather different in our day. For us, when we think "kingdom," we likely think of Walt Disney movies (where it's all sweet and sugary), or the United Kingdom (which is good for pomp and circumstance and TV specials but not exactly powerful), or places like Saudi Arabia (often accused of human rights violations). If God's kingdom is like any of those, we're not particularly interested.

But when Jesus's first hearers heard him say this, they would have caught their breath. They would be nervous and excited and hopeful—all at the same time. Can this possibly be true? Who is this who has the nerve to say this out loud in public? Who does he think he is?

And why would they react this way? Because all of their lives, and all of their parents' lives, and all of their grandparents' lives, they have been told a story, the story that one day this thing—God's kingdom—will come. They'd heard the story around the meal table and at the fireside in the evenings, in Sunday school (or the equivalent), and at bedtime: "One day God will get rid of all evil, suffering, and injustice and bring in a new world of compassion and joy." But it had never happened.

And now along comes this young guy from Nazareth, with no status, no training, no army, and not even any followers, saying, "OK, folks. You've been asking, How long, O Lord? When is this kingdom of yours going to come? When are you going to fix things? The answer is, 'This long.' God is done holding back. You don't have to wait any longer. The time is here right now. The kingdom is beginning now. The story is reaching its climax. Folks, this is good news, this is the gospel!"

Do you get the sense of what a crazy thing this is for him to say? The whole history of the world as the Jews understood it has come down to this single, solitary Galilean carpenter. And the people are thinking, "Are we going to believe him?"

They are right to be skeptical. It's easy for anyone to say, "The kingdom is at hand." Messiahs were common in those days, and none of them lasted very long. Indeed, most of them were crucified. So what does Jesus do to establish his credibility? He lives in a way that demonstrates the reality of God's kingdom. He heals the sick, raises the dead, feeds the hungry, and welcomes the marginalized. He forgives sins, shows his power over the forces of nature, and confronts the powers of oppression. As we watch Jesus at work, we see a small-scale model of what the world looks like when the Creator's love is expressed in everything, overcoming evil and creating wholeness. Jesus is the embodiment of the kingdom, the kingdom incarnate. If you want to know what God at work in the world looks like, look at Jesus. Which is not surprising, of course, since he is the king of this kingdom.

Think of it this way. When I was in high school in the UK, I remember learning about the reign of Elizabeth I in the sixteenth century. One of the quirky things about her reign is that during the summer months, she and her whole court (with a cast of hundreds) would leave London and visit some of her wealthier subjects around the country for long periods of time. This was not just the queen being gracious. Apart from anything else, it was a way for her to escape the summer heat of London. It also saved her a considerable expense—an expense that was conveniently transferred to her lords and ladies. You can be sure they groaned when they received the news that the queen was coming to stay for a month. It was a dubious and expensive privilege.

But here's the important point: you can bet that when they knew she was coming, they made absolutely sure that everything was done in the way Her Majesty preferred, whether it concerned her favorite foods, her preferred leisure activities, or the kind of music she liked. In other words, wherever the queen went, there was a microcosm of her kingdom. Everything was done in her way.

That's not a bad way to begin thinking about the kingdom of God. We can say that God's kingdom is

- where God is acknowledged as ruler and

- where things are therefore done in the way God likes,

- meaning it is a place of love, beauty, wholeness, justice, and joy.

- Likewise, it is a world where all sin and evil—whether racism, hunger, disease, injustice, or anything else—is eradicated.

- And as with Queen Elizabeth, the kingdom exists wherever the monarch goes.

In the kingdom of God, Jesus is king, and where he goes, the kingdom goes. As Dallas Willard puts it, "Jesus is the human face on the kingdom of God."[11]

This explains why all those personal statements about "good news for me" were so varied. They are among the myriad benefits that impact our lives when the kingdom of God comes along and touches us. (See figure 1.2.)

"The gospel," then, is simply the good news of what God is like, that God the Creator is on a mission to right all wrongs through Jesus Christ. It is the verbal explanation of what God is like and what God is doing through Jesus. If you like technical language, theologians use the Latin term *missio Dei* (mission of God) to describe this work of God in Jesus to restore all things.

One of my favorite images for the gospel is that of *kintsugi*, the Japanese art of repairing broken china with gold. Most of us, when trying to repair a beloved plate or dish, try to hide

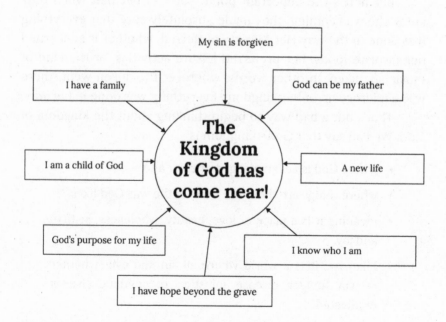

FIGURE 1.2. The kingdom of God has come near

the cracks so that the piece "looks like new." *Kintsugi* does the opposite: far from hiding the scars, it makes the broken places the highlight and the glory of the piece. Here's how one *kintsugi* master describes the process: "Kintsugi is not just fixing something and reusing it. It's a repair that creates something new— something unprecedented that is actually far more valuable than it was before. Kintsugi goes beyond restoration, to a new creation. It proves that something can be more beautifully broken and mended than it was before it even broke."[12]

I shared this analogy recently with a woman whose adult son had died of cancer. She in turn told me how she had been able to be of help to someone else with cancer because of that experience. Her scars were becoming something beautiful, a central part of her ministry.

God is the ultimate *kintsugi* master, and Jesus demonstrates how it works. An old hymn says, "Behold his hands and side, rich wounds, yet visible above, in beauty glorified."[13] Jesus is able to bring forgiveness and healing to us and our world not in spite of his scars but because of them. He is a savior with scars.

GOSPEL AND MISSION

Confession time. When I was putting this book together, I originally planned for a chapter about mission. But then the book began to take on a life and a coherent shape of its own without such a chapter, and I got worried. Was there some sinister, subconscious reason I didn't want to write about mission? Would people who are serious about mission (and there are a lot of them, thank God) dismiss the book out of hand because of the omission of mission? But as I looked over what I had written, the word *mission* appears in virtually every chapter, and (even more importantly) the idea of mission is very prominent even when the word isn't. What's this about?

Here's the reason I don't have a chapter about mission. The gospel and mission are conjoined twins. Or, more precisely, the idea of mission is nothing more than a fancy way of describing what the gospel is about. And the gospel is about the loving work of God in dealing with sin and evil while nurturing good in the world. Thus if you understand the gospel, you will understand mission. To put it another way, the gospel is the verbal announcement that God is on a mission to redeem and renew all things. Without the gospel to shape and guide it, "mission"—dealing with sin and evil while nurturing good—can become random do-goodery, which has little to do with the calling of the church. It is always dangerous to separate conjoined twins.

As I thought about this, I was reassured to observe that, in spite of how common it is in churches these days, the word *mission* is never used in the New Testament. The word *gospel*, on the other hand, is everywhere. The early Christians didn't need the word *mission*. They knew the gospel and sought to live it out. God had reached out in love to them, and they in turn reached out in love to the world.[14] That was enough.

So where did the idea of mission come from? The word *mission* in its modern sense of a particular orientation of church life was invented to highlight a growing weakness in the life of the church.[15] By the 1950s, the era of the church's dominance in the West—the time of Christendom—was over. A new era in the life of the church was beginning, an era in which the church would be small rather than big, weak rather than strong, nimble rather than inflexible, and concerned for the world rather than for its own welfare. Some have suggested that such a shift would be nothing less than a new Reformation, the kind of upheaval that only occurs about every five hundred years.[16] And the word *mission* was helpful in identifying this pivotal moment.[17]

All this is true. The word *mission* and its child *missional* have been helpful. But I would still contend that the primary need of the church is not to recapture a sense of mission—which too easily degenerates into a desperate search for survival techniques—but to be captured afresh by the good news of Jesus, the gospel, in all its splendor and magnetism.

CENTER AND CIRCUMFERENCE

All this means that the gospel is big—really big. It encompasses all of time and space. There is one place in the Bible that to my mind encompasses this bigness. It's a passage I used to read at the start of every course I ever taught at Wycliffe College. I chose it simply because it reminded me (and the students) of what the course just beginning was really about (whatever its title in the calendar), what the work of a seminary is about, what the life of the church is about—and indeed what the future of the world is all about. Listen to how Eugene Peterson translates Colossians chapter 1:

> We look at this Son and see the God who cannot be seen. We look at this Son and see God's original purpose in everything created. For everything, absolutely everything, above and below, visible and invisible, rank after rank after rank of angels—*everything* got started in him and finds its purpose in him. He was there before any of it came into existence and holds it all together right up to this moment. And when it comes to the church, he organizes and holds it together like a head does a body.
>
> He was supreme in the beginning and—leading the resurrection parade—he is supreme in the end. From beginning to end he's there, towering far above everything, everyone. So spacious is he, so roomy, that everything of God finds its proper place in him without crowding. Not only that, but all the broken and dislocated pieces of the universe—people and things, animals and atoms—get properly fixed and fit together in vibrant harmonies, all because of his death, his blood that poured down from the cross. You yourselves are a case study of what he does. (Col 1:15–21 MSG)

Do you notice how it begins and ends with Jesus? At the beginning, Jesus is the "cosmic Christ" who towers above all things and holds the universe together in love. And at the end is a picture of that same Jesus, but now dying on the cross in a specific place and time in history. He is both the circumference of the circle and its center.

Then notice the scope of Paul's vision. At its outer edges, it includes the restoration of "all the broken and dislocated pieces of the universe"—the broadest canvas possible. But at the heart of his vision are those very ordinary, struggling, "normal" Christians at Colossi, people like you and me, who are a "case study" of how this cosmic restoration works out on the ground. Who would have thought we and they were so important in the big scheme of things? But we are, we truly are.

If this is the right way to think about the gospel, there are some other places in Scripture that come into focus as summaries of the good news. How about these:

- Paul speaks of God's "plan for the fullness of time, to gather up all things in him, things in heaven and things on earth" (Eph 1:10). "Gathering up": it reminds me of Jesus's lovely image of his being a mother hen trying to gather her chicks into the safety of her wings (Matt 23:37). But here it is God gathering up everything in the universe.

- Or how about Peter's words in one of his sermons in Acts: "Jesus . . . must remain in heaven until the time of universal restoration that God announced long ago through his holy prophets" (Acts 3:20–21), or as the First Nations Version puts it, "The time comes when Creator will restore all things." Have you ever had a restoration project? A piece of old furniture, perhaps, or an old family photograph? How about God as the Ultimate Art Restorer, with this world as the work of art God is restoring?

- Jesus himself, in a passage it's easy to overlook, refers to "the renewal of all things" that is coming at the end of time (Matt 19:28). Everything. Renewed. Eventually. This is huge. How did we miss it?

I was sharing this with a church a few years back, and a woman, obviously quite distressed, came up to me in the break. "I always thought," she said, "that the gospel was about Jesus dying for our sins so we could be restored to a relationship with God. Am I wrong?" I felt terrible: How could what I had said possibly contradict what she had learned? "In Christ God was reconciling the world to himself" (2 Cor 5:19) is at the heart of the gospel. Of course. There would be no "renewal of all things" without the death and resurrection of Christ reconciling us to God. But at the same time, I could see how talk of God's work in renewing all things could look like "a different gospel." I did my best to say, "No, no, they are just different aspects of the same message." I don't know if she was convinced or if she just dismissed me as a heretic.

More recently, I came across a place where Tim Keller addresses this very tension. He puts it so much more clearly than I did:

> When we look at the whole scope of the [Christian] story line, we see clearly that Christianity is not only about getting one's individual sins forgiven so we can go to heaven. That is an important means of God's salvation, but not the final end or purpose of it. The purpose of Jesus's coming is to put the whole world right, to renew and restore the creation, not to escape it. It is not just to bring personal forgiveness and peace, but also justice and shalom to the world. God created both body and soul, and the resurrection of Jesus shows that he is going to redeem both body and soul. The work of the Spirit of God is not only to save souls but also to care [for] and cultivate the face of the earth, the material world.[18]

I wish I'd had that quote in my back pocket when the woman challenged me. It's not either/or but both/and: the microgospel and the macrogospel, the personal and the universal, Jesus dying for our sins and God making a new world. The cross is the key to the cosmic, not an alternative to it. We don't have to choose.

READING THROUGH THE LENS OF THE GOSPEL

Once we express the gospel in the "macro" kind of way, we can look back at those different statements of the gospel we were looking at earlier and see how they make better sense in this light:

- What about *John 3:16*, for a start? Here's a clue as to how this fits: John's Gospel uses the term "eternal life" where the other gospels say "kingdom." For John, they're the same thing. We could paraphrase him like this:

  1. God so loved the world that he gave his only son, so that

  2. whoever follows Jesus ("believes in him")

  3. should not be left outside of God's work to shape a new world ("perish")

  4. but take part in the work of God's kingdom—to renew all things—in this world and the next ("have eternal life").

- It shouldn't surprise us that the statement of the gospel in *Romans 1:3–4* mentions David. The prophets foretold a king "descended from David" because God's work through history is consistent: it has the Artist's distinctive style about it. So it is important that Jesus is a king descended from David: "The Davidic king is seen in some texts as the true Adam, and in others . . . as the fulfilment of the Abrahamic promises."[19]

- *First Corinthians 15:3–4* focuses on Jesus and his death for sins. Yes, of course. This was the price God paid at the hands of sinners who were determined to block the work of God. But it didn't work: the resurrection means not only that God's work cannot be stopped but that the new world has begun.

- And then, of course, there is *Galatians 3:8*. This odd statement of "the gospel beforehand" reflects Paul's conviction that God's restoration project did not begin with the coming of Jesus. In one sense, it began as soon as sin entered the world and God called out to Adam and Eve, "Where are you?" (Gen 3:9).[20] But in another it began with the call of Abraham and Sarah to be parents of a new nation, which would in turn be the incubator of the coming kingdom, which heralds the renewal of all things. So yes, Genesis 12 is indeed "the gospel" ahead of time.

If we put things this way, then we don't have to choose which of all these statements of "the gospel" is true. The gospel is so vast, so radical, so far-reaching that there could never be just one way of expressing it. Each statement is describing a different facet of a quite amazing diamond. Each one is stretching to contain the uncontainable—to describe something Paul says is actually "indescribable" (2 Cor 9:15)—and, unsurprisingly, not quite succeeding. As Rowan Williams says, "At the boundaries of speech, we are only at the beginning of the fullness of the gospel."[21]

Let's bring this home. What I've tried to do here is to move us from a very partial understanding of the gospel to a sense that it is actually a huge thing—bigger than we will ever grasp, perhaps, and certainly more than any of us can grasp right now.

WHY WE ARE BEGINNING HERE

When we think about Christian faith, where do we begin? You can make a case for beginning with God. After all, God is the source of all things.[22] Or you could argue that we have to begin with God's revelation in the Bible, which is where Christians learn what we know about God. Or what about Jesus—Jesus who is, after all, the key to understanding both God and the Bible?[23]

I am coming to the conclusion that the best place to begin is the subject of this chapter—the gospel.[24] It seems to me that the gospel is the best-focused lens through which to view God, the Bible, and Jesus. This is the starting point that sheds the clearest light—if you like, a "hermeneutical key"—for understanding Christian faith. Not that it is more important than those other things but that it makes the best sense to begin with this.

Of course, one could object that the gospel is not in fact articulated until almost the end of the Bible, whereas God is present from the beginning, and the Bible tells the story from the beginning. The gospel appears to be a Johnny-come-lately to the Bible story.

The answer is that the gospel is transhistorical.[25] Certainly it was articulated at a particular moment at the hinge of history, but the gospel then casts its light both forward and backward in time.

What could that possibly mean? The gospel sheds its light *forward*: once Jesus had articulated and demonstrated the gospel of God's love through his life, death, and resurrection, it began to move forward through history, changing the world as it went. And Christians believe that its impact will continue until God calls a halt to the march of time. There's the forward movement. Jesus's proclamation of the gospel jumpstarts a movement that is then catapulted forward through history.

But—and here is the tricky thing—the gospel also casts its light *backward* in time, as far as the beginning of the world, and even before that. How come? Because the gospel reveals the eternal heart of God. It tells us that *this* is what God is like and *this* is what God has always been like: compassionate, just, forgiving, healing, generous, and implacably opposed to anything that damages his beloved world. We can be misled by thinking that the work of Jesus on the cross changed God's attitude toward us—that he was mad at us beforehand but then decided to love us instead. But no. The cross, says Fleming Rutledge, "is the enactment *in history* of an *eternal* decision within the being of God."[26] I love the way Horace Bushnell expressed this: "There is a cross in God before the wood is seen on the hill. . . . It is as if there were a cross unseen, standing on its undiscovered hill, far back in the ages."[27] God's heart has always been one of love and compassion for this world—and the cross shows both that love and that opposition to evil.

Sometimes I have heard people say, "You can't have the good news until you have the bad news first." My answer has always been, "Well, Jesus didn't see it that way. His first message was the announcement of the good news, and only then did he talk about sin and repentance."[28] But now I think there's more to it than that. It is only when we are confronted with the good news of who God is that we realize the bad news of our condition without God and the need to do something about it. Once again, the gospel comes first.

In the rest of this book, I will try to show how, once we grasp this gospel of Jesus, it makes sense of everything else: what it means to be a Christian, what it means to be church, what it means to live in God's world. Let me try to show you how that works.

CHAPTER 2

THE GOSPEL, CONVERSION, AND BAPTISM

A Threefold Knot

Let's go back now to that dramatic scene on the beach in Mark chapter 1. Jesus is telling people that the kingdom is at hand, and their ears prick up. Can it be true? That God is about to turn the world right side up? That God will judge everything that is evil and restore all that is good? Is it possible? For them, that would mean that the ruling Romans will be defeated. After all, in their minds, the Roman Empire is the most obvious embodiment of the world's evil. And their nation will be restored to its rightful place as God's special people. That would truly be good news.

What now? There are two kinds of statements: those that are simply information ("Tigers live in India") and those that require action ("There's a tiger in the next room"). Jesus's announcement of the gospel is a statement of the second kind. It calls for a response. If this announcement is true—the kingdom is almost here—this is not just academic information. There are radical implications for us and for the whole human race, and they are summarized in two sharp and archaic words: *repent* and *believe* (see Mark 1:15).

Mark doesn't give us definitions of these two words. Instead, he immediately tells us the story of Jesus calling the first four disciples, two pairs of brothers named Simon and Andrew, James and John. Often these two stories—Jesus's announcement of the kingdom and the calling of the first disciples—are treated as two separate stories.[1] But I don't see them that way. If we see them as leading from the first into the second, what Mark is doing is giving us a real-life example of how people repent and believe, which is far more useful than a dictionary definition. How?

Well, let me show you what I mean by starting with what the dictionary says. Here is *repent*: the *Oxford English Dictionary* says to repent is "to feel or express sincere regret or remorse about one's wrongdoing or sin."[2] If people use the word *repent* at all in everyday life (which is seldom), it's often combined with the tongue-in-cheek phrase "in dust and ashes," which reinforces that idea of remorse for wrongdoing.

And what about *believe*—specifically, *believe in*? There are three possible meanings: one is to "have faith in the truth or existence of"; the second is "to be of the opinion that (something) is right or acceptable."[3] These two definitions often translate (in church life at least) into agreeing with a particular creed or set of beliefs. If you doubt me, check out church websites and notice the high proportion that include a tab along the lines of "What we believe." Now, I am a big fan of being clear about what you believe; there has always been an important place for that in the church. But it is not what Jesus means here.

If we follow those definitions, the first four disciples do not repent or believe. There is no evidence of turning from sin, nor of affirming belief in anything very specific—not even that Jesus is the Messiah. And without those two things, there would be no connection between Jesus's announcement and the calling of the disciples. Case closed.

But "repent" means literally "to change your mind"—to think differently about things, to turn from one state of mind to another.[4] And *believe* (in this context anyway) means something closer to the third dictionary definition: "to have confidence in (a person or a course of action)"—and thus to commit yourself, to give your allegiance to something (or someone). If you have confidence in someone, you trust them and are prepared to follow them.[5] Putting these two ideas together, it becomes clear that they are actually two halves of one whole: to turn away from one thing (repent) and to turn toward another (believe), a negative and a positive, together comprising a complete 180-degree U-turn.[6]

If there is a case to be made that these four men do in fact "repent and believe," it will be on the basis of understanding these words beyond their dictionary definitions. Let me put it this way. Until Jesus interrupted the lives of these four, they thought they knew what life was about. It meant taking care of your family, doing an honest day's work, being faithful to your wife, going to the synagogue on the Sabbath, and having a drink and a laugh with your friends. And of course, there's nothing wrong with those things. I think we are safe in assuming these four weren't exactly big-time sinners. Neither is Jesus asking that they give up cheating on their income tax (or the first-century equivalent), which we might consider a suitable subject for repentance. Frankly, that would be easy compared to what he is actually asking. No, these were just decent, ordinary working stiffs, minding their own business and getting on with their lives. Some people are identified in the Gospels as "sinners" needing repentance, but these four are not among them.

So what happens in this story? Basically, Jesus's announcement throws them off balance. If what he is saying is true, then life is not the way they thought it was. The whole orientation of their lives has been off kilter. Those things that have been the focus of their lives are not the most important things after all. There is something much bigger, something absolutely huge, going on: this thing Jesus calls the good news about the kingdom. If that is true, it's not a little corner of life called "religion"; it is everything. Jesus's abrupt "Follow me" is a call to a radically new life. What is important now is joining in with God's new work in the world. They are to "strive first for the kingdom of God and his righteousness" (Matt 6:33).

I would argue then that yes, the disciples do *repent*, in this deeper sense. Not by giving up specific bad habits, which is relatively easy (only relatively), but by changing their minds about what is important in life and reorienting their whole existence, which is a hundred times harder.

They also *believe*, in the sense that they "have confidence in" Jesus—or at least enough confidence to start walking the road with him (Mark 1:17, 20 FNV). As a result, nothing in their lives is ever the same again. It's as simple as that. And from now on, Mark calls them "disciples." That is their primary identity: not fishermen or husbands or citizens. Those are still true and important, but now they are secondary. They have become disciples, an identity that includes and transforms all those other identities.

New Testament scholar N. T. Wright points out that the ancient historian Josephus uses the words this same way. Josephus is urging a Jewish rebel leader to give up trying to defeat the Romans by military means: it's never going to work. Instead, the rebels should join Josephus in seeking a negotiated compromise. And how does Josephus word this invitation? "Repent and believe in me." Exactly the words Jesus used seventy years earlier. In both cases, this was an invitation not "to give up sinning and have a religious conversion experience" but rather to give up their preconceived ideas of how things should be and trust the speaker's way instead.[7]

Sometimes people say that the heart of sin is self-centeredness. Yet all of us know people who apparently have no religious convictions but who are deeply unselfish, so that can't be right. But what if we said sin is self-directedness? People can be unselfish and yet resist handing over the direction of their lives to God. (After all, what might God ask?) Conversely, selfish people can hand over the leadership of their lives and allow God to work on their self-centeredness. Not that transformation happens all at once, I admit, but becoming God-directed starts a journey away from sinful self-directedness. The ship has changed course and begun to head in a new direction. That is what is happening here.

I take these two neighboring stories—Jesus's announcement of the good news of the kingdom and the calling of the first disciples—as a model or paradigm for what Mark understands a Christian to be. So let's dig a little deeper into the idea of a disciple. What exactly does it mean for them and perhaps also for us?

WHAT IS A DISCIPLE?

In light of these stories, it's worth noticing that the first Christians didn't often call themselves Christians. The word is only used three times in the New Testament (Acts 11:26; 26:28; and 1 Pet 4:16), and on two of those occasions, it is a name given to them by other people, not a name they choose for themselves. Instead, the commonest term in the New Testament is this word *disciple*.[8]

This is hardly surprising. In many ways, Jesus fulfilled the role of a Jewish rabbi or teacher, and rabbis had disciples.[9] Thus he is often addressed as "rabbi" and seems comfortable with the title.[10] Even at the end of his earthly ministry, he is still using this term: "You call me Teacher and Lord—and you are right, for that is what I am" (John 13:13). Not surprisingly, then, his first followers were referred to as his "disciples." Of course, over time they came to realize that Jesus was more than a teacher—much more—but he was never *less* than a teacher. And the implication of being a disciple of Rabbi Jesus is that he is founding a school.[11]

First, then, what does it mean to be a disciple? The most literal meaning of the word is "learner." For a long time, I thought it was helpful to say that a disciple is a student. And it's not untrue, except that in much of the world, "student" often means a young person sitting in a row with other students, listening and taking notes while a teacher at the front gives a lecture. (You may know that old definition of a lecture as the means by which the teacher's notes become the students' notes without passing through the minds of either.) And although Jesus seems to have done some lecturing, like the Sermon on the Mount (though I rather doubt the Twelve took notes, and I'm quite sure their minds were engaged), that wasn't the main way the disciples learned.

What the disciples experienced was closer to what we would call an apprenticeship. I was once asked to preach about this in my own home church and had a brainwave. Instead of pontificating about what apprenticeship means, I invited my friend Ken to come up from the congregation so that I could interview him. Ken is an electrician. The interview really only had one question: "So, Ken, how did you learn to be an electrician?" The answer was, "Well, on Mondays, we went to class and had lectures about electronics. Then, from Tuesday to Friday, we were out on the job with a master electrician and learned in a hands-on kind of way how to be electricians." And the end result of this training was to create not an expert on theoretical electronics but someone who was (and is) a very competent professional electrician.

That's the parallel with how Jesus taught his disciples. Yes, there was talking, but there was also plenty of action, and the two were integrated. And the end of the process was not a bunch of people with answers to every theoretical question about God and the Bible but graduates of an informal three-year apprenticeship.

Of course, this unstructured approach raises the question of what this school is for. It's clear what electrician school is about, but what about Jesus's school? Well, Peter and Andrew, James and John, became disciples after they heard the good news about the kingdom, so there must be an intrinsic connection between these two things. Let's think of it this way: the school of Jesus is where disciples learn the ways of the kingdom, what it means to experience and live good news. Repentance and belief mean you leave whatever school or schools you were in before and commit to being a full-time apprentice under Jesus's tutelage. The community of Jesus's apprentices thus forms a trade school where people are trained in kingdom living.

When you think about it, isn't this what is going on in the rest of the Gospels? The disciples are following Jesus around, watching him at work, listening to him talk, asking him questions, and being asked (much harder) questions in return, and little by little, they are initiated into the work of the kingdom. They see Jesus at work, healing, exorcizing, feeding, loving, confronting evil, challenging hypocrisy—foreshadowing the cross by daily laying down his life—and they see how these things are good news for those he meets.

But Jesus has a plan to make them more than passive spectators. They will become not just observers of the gospel: the gospel will begin to change them, and they will themselves become agents of the gospel.

You may be familiar with that simple summary of how training works: I *do, you watch. I do, you help. You do, I help.* And finally, *You do, I watch.* Take the story of the feeding of the five thousand (Mark 6:35–44). In much of the story to this point, it's been a case of I *do, you watch.* But now the balance of responsibility shifts. When the day is drawing to a close, and the crowd is getting hungry, the Twelve make recommendations as to what Jesus should do. *You do it, we'll watch.* They like it that way. But he turns to them and says, in effect, "I'm not going to solve this for you; it's your turn." It looks as if this has suddenly turned into a *You do, I'll watch* scenario. To the disciples' relief, I'm sure, it turns into a *I'll do, you help* situation.[12] Jesus does the miracle, but the disciples look after the administration and (I'm sure) enjoy the reflected glory. They are still the junior partners in the enterprise, certainly, but it's a big step forward in their apprenticeship.

By the end of the gospel story, when Jesus leaves them, they are hardly 100 percent qualified to take over the work of the kingdom—that much is clear—but one of the very lessons they were supposed to have learned was that the kingdom is for those who understand that they're likely to fail and know what to do when that happens.

If we understand the disciples' experience through this lens of the trade school, it means that Jesus's parting words, "Go, make disciples," can be understood as "Go and put others through the same kind of training program that you had. Invite others into this process of learning about the kingdom and becoming agents of the gospel." In order to understand what he means, we have to look back over the three years that the disciples were with Jesus to see how he shaped them.[13] Now, having started his trade school where apprentices learned the skills of the kingdom, he sends the first graduates out to start "satellite campuses" and do what they saw him do, wherever they go.[14]

If they had received a certificate at the end of the three years, it would have said something like this:

This is to certify that

Simon Peter of Galilee

has spent three years in the school of Jesus,

interacted with Jesus on a daily basis,
watched him, listened to him,

asked questions, and tried to
answer Jesus's questions.

He has some experience of doing the
same kind of work as Jesus.

Once he has received the power of the
Holy Spirit, in the opinion of Jesus,

Simon Peter will be qualified to lead
others to learn the ways of Jesus.

What the four fishermen begin on that fateful day is an apprenticeship to Jesus. He is the Master Craftsman, and his disciples are learning his "trade" from him.

You may be thinking, "I've never heard this idea of Jesus heading up a trade school. What's that about? Does it still exist?" There is of course a familiar word by which we usually refer to this school: it's called the church. I would argue that the heart of church is the group of people who follow in the footsteps of the first disciples to learn the way of Jesus. The church is those who, like the fishermen,

- have heard Jesus's announcement of the kingdom and recognize it as good news about what God is doing in the world;

- respond to the message with repentance and faith, knowing that this is the greatest reality in the world, which therefore demands all that they are and have;

- commit their lives to being apprentices of Jesus and learning the ways of the kingdom;

- are being slowly shaped by the kingdom values of death to self and resurrection;
- are influencing the world around them in the ways of the kingdom; and
- are recruiting others to join the school ("fish for people").

I suggested at the end of the previous chapter that the Christian faith and everything it involves—being a Christian, being the church, living in God's world—can all be understood (indeed, are *best* understood) through the lens of the gospel, and here is the first example. Jesus announces the gospel—the good news that God is at work to right the world—and immediately invites people to be his apprentices in this work. If we equate "being a disciple" and "being a Christian" (and I do), the link immediately makes sense.

The church, which is at its heart the community of Jesus's apprentices, grows out of the gospel. Indeed, we could say that the gospel is a seed whose fruit is called church. Without the gospel, there would be no church. Church is the gospel in full flower.[15] But "the church" is not an abstract thing; neither is it in the first place a worldwide institution. At its heart it is simply the trade school of Jesus's apprentices.

This is why it is such a tragedy when church folk—let alone those outside the church—do not know what the gospel is. If you asked a member of Amnesty International, or a volunteer for the Cancer Society, or a nurse working with Doctors without Borders (DWB) what their organization was about and they couldn't tell you, how long would those organizations survive? The reason people support Amnesty is their concern for those who are unjustly imprisoned. Of course! People collect money for cancer (usually) because of a close personal encounter with cancer, either their own or that of a loved one. Naturally. People get involved with DWB because they care about people in countries without adequate medical care. And in each case, those involved would be able to explain the purpose of their organization. It seems obvious, doesn't it?

Well, yes; but why are people involved in church? Why do they call themselves Christians? Should this not be equally obvious?

Unless we can give a clear and succinct answer to this question, I suggest it will be difficult to sustain our personal faith, let alone the church.

There is one more thing that needs to be said about gospel and discipleship, and it has to do with baptism.

BAPTISM

The road from gospel to discipleship and church passes through a doorway called baptism. Baptism is intimately connected to Jesus's preaching of the gospel and his call to "repent and believe," his call to conversion.

Now, I am aware that talking about conversion as an event can make some people nervous, just as the concept of baptism as a sacrament alarms others. Urban Holmes pointed out some years ago that "historically, those Christians who have emphasized the sacraments have put very little emphasis upon conversion, and those who have sought conversion have had a weak sacramental theology."[16]

Conversion, especially in mainline denominations, often prompts a defensive response: "Ah, but I try to be converted every day, not just once." Of course, this argument makes an important point: discipleship is a daily discipline, not just a long-ago date in our autobiography. Yet the issue is not so easily resolved, since there is a sacrament of conversion, and it is called baptism. If conversion were a daily thing, we would need to be baptized daily! This is why people sometimes refer to the Christian life as "living out our baptism."

Let's go back to the idea of the school. We can think of baptism this way: baptism is how we register in the trade school of Jesus.[17] What we do day by day is try to live out our apprenticeship.

Baptism has many layers of symbolism, which is why it's so powerful in conveying how rich and multifaceted a thing it is to become a Christian. For instance, the water is a symbol of cleansing—in this case, cleansing from sin, our life apart from God's leadership. Water is also a symbol of birth, of emerging from the womb. This relates to Jesus's idea that to become a Christian is to be "born again." But most importantly (and this doesn't relate so much to sprinkling with water, though that has its own symbolism), going under the water symbolizes a death and a resurrection—leaving behind the old life and beginning a new and resurrected life with Jesus.

Every church tradition does baptism slightly differently. But certainly with adult baptisms, the person to be baptized is generally asked to confirm that they understand what they are doing. In churches where babies are baptized, the sponsors or godparents make such statements. In either tradition, some churches use a set liturgy of questions and answers divided neatly into two halves, the first negative and the second positive. Here is one example:

> Do you renounce Satan and all the spiritual forces of wickedness that rebel against God? I *renounce them.*
>
> Do you renounce the evil powers of this world, which corrupt and destroy the creatures of God? I *renounce them.*
>
> Do you renounce all sinful desires that draw you from the love of God? I *renounce them.*
>
> Do you turn to Jesus Christ and accept him as your Saviour? I *do.*
>
> Do you put your whole trust in his grace and love? I *do.*
>
> Do you promise to obey him as your Lord? I *do.*[18]

It's not rocket science to figure out that these two sets of questions represent the two halves of Jesus's invitation to discipleship: first the "repenting" (what we turn away from) and then the "believing" (what we turn to). To be baptized is to commit to being a disciple. When we are baptized, we are agreeing to set aside our own petty agendas and dreams for our lives—to die to those things—and to enter into the work of God's new world, the work of the gospel. By baptism, we commit to live as apprentices of Jesus.

We often say "blood is thicker than water." But in the case of baptism, as one author puts it, "Water is thicker than blood."[19] The water of baptism marks our being made an apprentice of Jesus and submitting our lives to his mentoring. The blood of family and all earthly ties now give way to the demands of God's kingdom.

Not that those ties are trivial or unimportant, but after baptism we engage with those things from the perspective of God's kingdom instead of viewing God's kingdom from the perspective of our earthly commitments. This is why missiologist Lesslie Newbigin says, to be baptized is "to be baptized into [God's] mission."[20] God's mission—the work of God in our lives and in the world—becomes the driving force of our lives from this point onward.[21]

GETTING PERSONAL

So what does all this have to say to us today? In one sense, nothing has changed since the first disciples: the heart of being a Christian is still being an apprentice of Jesus Christ, learning from him how to live the ways of his kingdom.

May I be personal for a moment? This stuff about discipleship is not an academic study, nor a theoretical subject. The good news Jesus announced is still good news. If you look at the problems of the world, it is clear that "someone ought to do something" about it. The central Christian conviction is that "someone" is indeed doing "something": the Creator of all things is working to do something—indeed, everything that needs doing—through Jesus Christ. And this God also chooses to work through human beings to do the work of putting the world to rights.

There are many ways of expressing these truths. (Remember figure 1.1 in chapter 1, the circle with the arrows indicating all the different things that drew people to discipleship?) Here's one that seems to connect with a lot of people. Maybe it will speak to you.

A few years ago, I was in downtown Toronto meeting with a group of young people who were curious about the Christian faith. They had talked with Christian friends and had questions. Early on, I asked them, "What do you think the heart of Christian faith is?" One said, "Oh, it's all about accepting-Jesus-Christ-as-your-personal-Lord-and-Savior." (He made it sound like a single word.) Another said, "Well, we're all sinners, but Jesus died for our sins, so if we confess our sins, we'll be forgiven." A third said, with a roll of the eyes, "Well, it's all about worshipping God. Though why God needs to be worshipped, I really don't know." What was intriguing to me was that although each of those answers is good news in a way, not one of these people sounded very excited about what they'd heard. None of them seemed to have heard it as "good news."

Then (as I confess I had hoped) they asked me, "So what do you think Christianity is all about?" I said, "Actually, I think it's all about joy. God loves us and wants to fill the world with joy. But every day, you and I do things to mess up God's plan so that the world is not filled with joy. But God says, 'If you give up your self-directed life and follow Jesus, I will begin to fill your life with joy, and through you the whole world.'"

There was a silence, and then one said, "I've never heard that before." Another one said, "I kinda like it."

Thinking back to that occasion, I realize I could have said, "God wants to fill the world with love" or "God wants to fill the world with peace." But I suspect those would have sounded too much like clichés—even though they are true. The idea of joy, on the other hand, still seems to touch people in a fresh and attractive way.

You may ask (I even hope you will), "But where are sin and repentance and faith and the kingdom and discipleship in that—all those things you've been talking about?" The answer, of course, is that they are present, but in other words:

- a world full of joy is what Jesus calls "the kingdom,"
- sin is all the ways in which we are obstacles to joy—our self-directedness,
- "repent and believe" are wrapped up in that phrase "if you follow Jesus,"
- personal change is God restoring joy in us, and
- engaging with God's mission in the world is God bringing joy to others through us.

Is this all that needs to be said about the gospel and the Christian life? No, of course not. Apart from anything else, there is nothing about the cost of discipleship and taking up your cross—although that would follow very naturally. But for many, this way of putting things may be a point where the gospel gets traction in their imaginations; it may be a starting point on the journey to Christ and discipleship. It's rather like telling a child that a mommy and daddy make a baby. Is it the whole truth? Of course not. But it's the truth stated in an elementary kind of way, and fuller explanations can be added bit by bit as the child is ready. The same with discipleship. This is a school, remember.

Here's the personal bit: Have you responded to Jesus's invitation? Perhaps you have heard the message and have said, "Yes!" As an apprentice of Jesus, you are aware of how he is working to change you and how you are working with him on the kingdom tasks he has given you. That's great.

But perhaps you are not an apprentice and you know you are not. Perhaps you are reading this book simply because you are concerned about the future of the church—and this idea of committing ourselves to Jesus as apprentices in his kingdom is not the kind of answer you expected.

One bishop told me she had been preaching about discipleship at a church in her diocese. After the service, a longtime member came up to her, very irate, and said, "I am *not* a disciple: I am a *member!*" Well, I'm glad he knew the difference. Perhaps you feel that way. You may consider yourself a churchgoer or a religious person—neither of them bad things, of course—but you've never thought of church and membership in this way. It's new and disturbing—but at the same time quite exciting. I understand that ambivalence.

But if this way of looking at things is right, it's not just food for thought; it's food for action. As Dallas Willard explains it, "The final step in becoming a disciple is decision. We become a life student of Jesus by deciding. . . . We should apprentice ourselves to Jesus in a solemn moment, and we should let those around us know that we have done so."[22]

Today, we have an opportunity to say yes to Jesus and his invitation to apprentice with him and, in the process, to play our part in restoring joy to the world. Saying yes to Jesus—however tentatively—is really all we have to do. It's the simplest and most awesome prayer we can ever pray.

CHAPTER 3

THE GOSPEL AND DISCIPLESHIP
Three Tools of the Trade

All apprenticeships are demanding. Worthwhile skills can't be learned overnight. After all, if you want to be a plumber, one website I discovered says that it will require "a five-year apprenticeship, ten thousand hours plus 744 hours of class room studies . . . and then work for a master plumber for five years, and once you have ten years documented time in, then you can take the four-part masters exams."[1] Many other training programs have similar requirements.

Exactly how long does an apprenticeship to Jesus take, then? As you can tell, this training is not a thing that can be accomplished just by reading a book on the topic or by a twelve-week classroom course or even a yearlong study group—although all of those may help. There are no shortcuts. Training in the trade school of Jesus is a process that takes our whole lives and requires a daily, 24/7 commitment to put one foot in front of the other on the road of learning. The school of Jesus requires what Friedrich Nietzsche called "a long obedience in the same direction."[2]

Let me say a word more about what the school is for. We have said it's the place where we are trained by Jesus for the work of the kingdom. But I wouldn't want that to be misunderstood. School does not just equip us to change the world, although it does that. School also changes us, and at the deepest level.

I suspect this is different from most other kinds of apprenticeship. You can learn to be a perfectly competent plumber without your character being changed. If you were a kind person when you began your apprenticeship, hopefully you are still so by the end. If you were a jerk when you began, well, I don't think there is anything intrinsic to a plumbing apprenticeship that will change that. But in the school of Jesus, personal change is right there at the heart of the learning.

Years ago, I knew a couple that had adopted twins, and the twins were proving to be quite a handful. One day, while I was visiting, one of the twins came in from the yard where she had been playing with a friend and said to her father, "Daddy, was I adopted or adapted?" He said with a wry smile, "You were adopted, sweetheart; we're still working on the adapting." That's central to what the school of Jesus is about: God adopts us through Christ (Eph 1:5) and then gradually adapts us to the life of this new community—this new family—where everyone is being changed to be like Jesus.

How does this work, then? This is a huge topic, because the gospel touches every area of life. This shouldn't surprise us, of course: God created all of life, sin has polluted every area of life to a lesser or greater extent, and so the gospel of Christ restores all of life. It's that simple—and that radical.

Because it's such a huge topic, there are lots of things I'm not going to talk about—and that may frustrate you: suffering, money, sex, the workplace, art, or politics. Any or all of these may be part of the life of a disciple. But others better qualified have written on those topics. (The books haven't quite filled the world yet, but we're getting there.)

Having said that, I have noticed that there are a few underlying principles that are crucial, whatever area of life God may be working on in our lives. You will see (once again) that each one is organically connected to the gospel of Jesus—how we experience it and enjoy it and how we express it. Let's begin with the first one.

1. COMMUNITY: YOU CAN'T BE A DISCIPLE BY YOURSELF

I once did research into the question of why Christian young people stay within the Christian faith as they grow up.[3] In my survey, among various options, I invited them to identify themselves in one of two ways: "I still consider myself a Christian, and I'm involved in church" or "I still consider myself a Christian, but I'm no longer involved in church." I was explaining this to a Sikh friend, and he asked in some surprise, "Why does it matter whether they're involved in church or not? Surely the important thing is whether they're still Christians?"

The answer is, it depends what kind of religion we're talking about, because they're all different. (In fact, I don't find *religion* a terribly helpful word.) In Buddhism, for example, I understand that nobody *has* to go to the temple or meet with other Buddhists for worship. In theory, you could be a solitary Buddhist all of your life and not miss out.

Christianity is very different. Remember that it has its origin in the good news that Jesus preached and lived—that God is seeking to repair everything in the world that is broken through sin. One of those things God wants to restore is human community—and church is one of the key places this is supposed to happen.

Why is this so important? Here's another way to express the gospel: the world was intended to reflect the character of its Creator. All works of art embody something of the character of the artist, and the world is no exception. But part of the nature of God, as the church has come to understand it, is that God is community—the community of the Trinity. Therefore, one aspect of the gospel is that, through Jesus, God is working to restore the kind of community that exists within the Trinity—a community of love, dynamism, and cooperation.

What might that look like on a human scale? J. R. R. Tolkien once wrote that *The Lord of the Rings* was "a fundamentally religious and Catholic work."[4] One of the ways the Christian subtext shows itself is in what the story says about community. If you know the story, you will be aware that "the fellowship of the ring" consists of three hobbits, two men, one dwarf, and one elf. These are races that normally have little to do with one another. Indeed, in the case of dwarves and elves, there is a long-standing history of suspicion and distrust. Yet in this story, they are called to work together for the common good. Legolas the elf and Gimli the dwarf in particular become fast friends, appreciating one another's strengths and able to tease one another about their differences. There is true community.

The forces of the Ring, on the other hand—Sauron, Saruman, Wormtongue, and the orcs—are always fighting among themselves and seem to find cooperation impossible. Evil seems to drive people apart and destroy community; good pulls them together. The one is centripetal, the other centrifugal.[5]

So one of the lessons in the school of Jesus, which we generally call church, is simply to be with other apprentices of Jesus. That is in itself one part of the learning and the changing that is the apprenticeship. Simply being in a church community and hanging in there through thick and thin, watching how others express their faith, learning to work alongside people we don't necessarily see eye to eye with—and even learning to love them—that's part of our apprenticeship. We challenge, encourage, teach, and (basically) love one another into the ways of the kingdom.

It doesn't really matter where we find a Christian community, where we are known and can grow in discipleship, whether it is in person or online, home Bible study groups, one-on-one "spiritual friendships," intentional communities (where people share a house), women's breakfasts, groups that come together to serve— there are a thousand variations—but if we are to move ahead in our apprenticeship, we will need to find it somewhere.

Unfortunately, just showing up on a Sunday morning is probably not the best way to develop this kind of relationship. In some ways, as my friend Bruxy Cavey puts it, "Sunday morning is a dietary supplement."[6] It is all too easy to show up for church, engage in worship, and then leave. But that is not community, certainly not the kind of community that transforms. Something more is needed.

2. THE BIBLE: DISCIPLES NEED TO BE SHAPED BY GOD'S STORY

During the COVID-19 crisis in 2020, as Christians tried to come to terms with why God had allowed this to happen and asked where God was in the pandemic, many instinctively turned to the Bible. Some went back to the story of Jesus being asleep in the boat during the storm on the Sea of Galilee and being woken up just in time to stop it (Luke 8:23–25). One drew on the experience of Mary, who, having been told by Gabriel that her life was about to be turned upside down in disturbing and painful ways, responds by singing, "My soul magnifies the Lord" (Luke 1:46–47). One of the more imaginative references was to the celebration of the dedication of Solomon's Temple, which is followed immediately by God's warning of drought, locusts, and plague and what to do in such circumstances (2 Chr 7:13–14). And I'm sure there were countless others.

Why is this significant? These are dramatic examples of how Christians try to "find themselves" in the stories—and *the* story—of the Bible. These stories help when we are struggling to make sense of what has happened in our lives, trying to relate to God in these new circumstances, and figuring out how to live our lives faithfully. They give stability, a measure of peace, and hope.

There can be no discipleship without the Bible. Does that sound narrow-minded? Perhaps it is, but (you may be shocked to know) narrow-mindedness is not always a bad thing. Let me explain. We could say for a start that the Bible is the textbook for our apprenticeship, the map for our journey, and the spiritual history of our family. All those images are true, but the Bible is also more than any of these.

We all live by stories. Stories help us understand the world and our place in it. Kurt Vonnegut has a short story in which the main character is utterly colorless until he is taking part in a play, when he comes stunningly alive. A female actor takes an interest in him and quickly realizes that the only way to have a meaningful relationship with him is by taking the female lead opposite him. But how can they continue to relate once they are outside the walls of the theater? By continuing to read plays to one another. When they can do that, the relationship flourishes. Finally, at the end of the story, the producer approaches the couple about acting in a new play. The woman's first question is, "Who am I this time?"[7]

We take our identity from the stories we take part in. As philosopher Alasdair MacIntyre once wrote, "I can only answer the question, 'What am I to do?' if I can answer the prior question, 'Of what story or stories do I find myself a part?'"[8]

So what story do apprentices of Jesus find themselves a part of? The story out of which Jesus himself lived: the story of the Bible. How can such a thing be? What could it possibly mean to "live out of the Bible's story"?

I have been helped in thinking about this by an image invented by N. T. Wright. He says, "Suppose there exists a Shakespeare play, most of whose fifth act has been lost." Everybody is excited to see this previously unknown play. So what can be done? It would be possible, I suppose, to commission some great Shakespearean scholar to write the missing act. But Wright suggests it would be "better . . . to give the key parts to highly trained, sensitive, and experienced Shakespearean actors, who would immerse themselves in the first four acts . . . *and who would then be told to work out a fifth act for themselves.*"[9]

What then will the actors do? They cannot simply go and look up the right answers. Nor can they just imitate the kinds of things that their particular character did in the earlier acts. The story Shakespeare wrote gives a framework and a direction for working out act 5 but does not dictate it. On the one hand, the actors will need to be faithful to the characters and plotlines Shakespeare created—otherwise, the story will lack coherence. But on the other hand, the actors also have freedom as to how they develop those characters and work out those plots.

They will speak and act, says Wright, "with both innovation and consistency."[10] This, he suggests, is the attitude apprentices of Jesus should have to the Bible. It is the Christian's authority in the same sense that acts 1 through 4 of the play are the actors' authority.

What are those acts? Act 1 is the story of creation—God's invention of a good and beautiful world. Act 2 is where things go wrong: where we choose to do things our way instead of the Creator's. In act 3, the Creator starts over, beginning to shape the

Hebrew people into a community that will be a microcosm of how human community should live in God's world.[11] Then, in act 4, the Creator enters into the story as one of the characters, to live and die and rise again for us.

Brian Walsh and Richard Middleton have suggested that this analogy can be strengthened by the addition of a sixth act (even though Shakespeare's plays inconveniently have only five).[12] So what is act 6? This is when the curtain finally comes down: all the loose ends are tied up, virtue is rewarded and evil abolished, and "God may be all in all" (1 Cor 15:28).

And yes, I do realize I skipped act 5, and you know why. Act 5 is where we are right now. We are not making up the story by which we live; rather, we are living in God's story. "Who am I this time?" This time, I am God's person learning to live in God's world. But that doesn't mean living by a rigid script. There is form, but there is also freedom. There is freedom, but it has direction and purpose. One friend calls this "faithfully improvising God's story," and those two words—*faithfully* and *improvising*, like Wright's *innovation* and *consistency*—carry equal weight. Thus the Bible will not give us a simple answer to the question of what to do about (say) genetically modified foods, but it will give us enough guidance from the other acts of the play to figure it out.

Or think of it this way. The story of the Bible is the story of the gospel. Through all its subplots and sidebars flows the central current of a story about God—*the* story about God. The Bible is the big story of God's gospel at work in the world, from beginning to end. And within that big story are many smaller stories of how God shaped people in the ways of the kingdom for thousands of years before we ever came along—Abraham and Sarah, Moses, Deborah, David, Ruth, and so many others. We read those stories of their successes (a few), their failures (many), and their wrestling with God. And we see how each of those personal stories was woven into the big story of God's work in the world.

As I have already said, Jesus's first disciples knew this story—and the stories within the story—very well. Indeed, being Jewish, they were born into a world shaped by it. That story shaped their understanding of what life was all about: work, worship, family, sexuality, right and wrong, the past and the future—everything. In our culture, we might say it formed their worldview. And that story formed the background against which the Twelve came to understand who Jesus was and what he was doing. When he said "kingdom" or "Son of Man" or "in that day," they did not need a Bible encyclopedia to understand what he meant. Those terms were part of the story that was in their lifeblood, which shaped their minds and hearts.

So let's move to today. Everybody lives within a story. The story of Scripture shaped the lives of Jesus and the Twelve. But today our culture tells lots of stories about the world, and frequently they compete for our loyalty with the God story. Some are stories about the importance of self-fulfillment ("Follow your dreams!"), others are stories of playing it safe ("America first!"), and yet others are stories of how to feel powerful ("Believe in yourself!"). As a result, followers of Jesus need to be reminded every day—or, when you think how often the other stories bombard us, perhaps every five minutes is more appropriate—of what story we truly belong to, of the story that can guide the human race into ways of vitality and true flourishing.

Here's an example. One of the most popular stories in our culture is what I think of as the Walt Disney myth: "You can be anything you want to be." Frankly, nothing in the Christian story would support this slogan: it is unrealistic and unkind. Blogger Diana Hartman responds to the suggestion that you can be whatever you want to be: "No, you can't. If that were true there would be a lot fewer janitors and a lot more astronauts. . . . The idea that we're all born with an unlimited list of occupational possibilities to pursue is a heartless assertion to foist upon children and a set-up for adults."[13] The Christian story would say instead something like this: "You can become whatever your loving Creator has gifted you to be. Follow Jesus and let his Spirit develop your unique character and your gifts." And that story leads to life.

This is why I say there can be no discipleship without the Bible. Now you understand why I said it is narrow-minded—and that's not a bad thing. If you think Jesus is worth following. It is no more narrow-minded than saying, "Without oxygen, there can be no life." It is just the nature of reality.

Having said that, *how* we get to know the Bible and live in its story is secondary. Personal reading and reflection are basic. Listening to good preaching that explains the Bible helps greatly. Reading and discussing a chapter with a friend over coffee every couple of weeks makes a difference. Working with Scripture in a regular small group is great. I have done all of these at one time or another, and they have changed my life. All of them amount to this: trying to be aware as we live our lives of those moments when secular stories challenge the God story and deliberately choosing to follow the latter.

Simply hearing Bible readings at church for five minutes every week is hardly going to shape our characters as disciples. Neither is it enough to counteract the stories that insinuate their way into our hearts and minds as we go about our daily lives on the other six days. The story of the Bible has to get into our heads and our hearts, and thence it has to shape our wills, our choices, and our commitments.

3. PRAYER: BEING OPEN TO GOD'S WORK

I find prayer a problem. If you don't, you can skip this section.[14] Not long ago, I was asked to be on the board of a prayer ministry in my city, the local chapter of 24/7, the worldwide prayer movement. I thought about it, then said to the director who invited me, "As long as you understand that I know less about prayer than I did fifty years ago." He thought that would be OK. He may yet regret it.

Why is prayer a problem for me? Well, for some people, it seems to be easy, simply a matter of living in God's presence and communicating with God as simply and regularly as breathing. For others, it seems like very hard work, involving long nights of prayer and periods of fasting. I find it difficult to identify completely with either of these, though I have experienced both.

Maybe it would help to go back to first principles. As through-out this book, my interest is not particularly in giving practical advice. There are lots of good resources for that out there. Instead, I want to pull back and think about the basic principles underlying the whole idea of prayer and how we pray. In particular, if my thesis holds that the gospel shapes and underlies everything in Christian theology and living, I want to see how that might apply to prayer.

The Gospel Opens the Way to God

The gospel is that God is making all things new through Christ. One of those things is that our relationship with God is restored.

A long trail called the Bruce Trail is just steps from our house, and on many days of the week, my wife, Deborah, and I begin the day by walking for twenty or thirty minutes along "our" bit of the trail.[15] But during the COVID-19 pandemic, we were denied access to our beloved trail and to so many other places. You probably remember similar restrictions, and if so, you will also remember the absolute delight when access was restored.

"Access" is one of those things we take for granted—but we shouldn't. Look at how excited the apostle Paul gets about the idea of access, this time access to God:

- "I thank God for your lives of free and open access to God, given by Jesus" (1 Cor 1:4 MSG).

- Through him we both [Jews and gentiles] share the same Spirit and have equal access to the Father (Eph 2:16–18 MSG).

Paul is so aware from his own experience how a self-directed life (and in his case, it was religiously self-directed, which is perhaps worse) makes access to the loving presence of God impossible. And he is equally clear that this new access is "given by Jesus," through his death on the cross. It is Jesus's death that has removed the barrier to the spiritual trail so that we have "free and open access to God."

I am aware that some people get antsy at the use of a phrase like "a personal relationship with Jesus" or "a personal relationship with God." The phrase is a relatively new one in the history of the church, so most Christians in history have managed quite well without it. Yet I believe it does sum up a key aspect of the good news: we human beings, in spite of our sinful ways, have access to "a personal relationship with Jesus."

And this is not the preserve of conservative evangelical Christians. I recall a doctoral seminar in which the students were reading an article critiquing the whole personal relationship idea. It's not difficult to do: the concept is individualistic (Whatever happened to the church?), it encourages private faith (just me and Jesus), it's pietistic (encouraging separation from involvement in the world), and so on. Then one of the students thought to ask the professor, a very senior Jesuit academic, what he thought of the article. "I felt very sorry for the author," he replied.

Whether or not we use the phrase, the reality it represents is wonderful. Yes, it needs to be in the context of the church's relationship with God through Jesus and of corporate worship (as of course it is for the Jesuits). Yes, it needs to lead us to involvement in God's world, not withdrawal from it (again, as the Jesuits well know). But Jesus's death has broken down the barrier between us and God: let's enter in boldly and enjoy being in the presence of God!

At the same time, like all "personal relationships," this one needs nurturing through communication, and one thing prayer does is give us an environment for communication with God. I didn't quite say "prayer is communicating with God," because it's more than that. Here's one part of that "more."

The Gospel and Prayer Change Us

Relationships change us. Those closest to us, whether family or friends, colleagues or fellow churchgoers, draw out some things in our characters and cause us to repress others. There is scientific evidence that couples grow to look alike the longer they are together. The person doing this research concluded that "people, often unconsciously, mimic the facial expressions of their spouses in a silent empathy and that, over the years, sharing the same expressions shapes the face similarly."[16] Is it too whimsical to suggest that as we spend time in the presence of God, seeking to feel as God feels about the world—finding joy in the things that delight God and feeling grief at the things that break God's heart—the more we grow like God? Paul obviously believed something like this: "Nothing between us and God, our faces shining with the brightness of his face. And so we are transfigured much like the Messiah, our lives gradually becoming brighter and more beautiful as God enters our lives and *we become like him*" (2 Cor 3:18 MSG; italics mine).

Here's one way I have experienced a little of this—and it took me by surprise. One of my Lenten disciplines for the past few years has been to pray particularly for people I find difficult, something I try to do daily during Lent. (You may be glad to know that it's a short list, and you're not on it.) Naturally, when I first began to do this, my prayer was that God would smooth out some of those characteristics in them that I found so irritating. After all, God must find them irritating too—right? Well, you can probably foresee where this is going.

Slowly, things that were good about them began to come to mind. I thought, "Come on, Lord, don't change the subject." I also found my mind straying uncomfortably to exactly what it was in me that found them irritating and the fact that they might find me equally or more (gasp!) difficult. (How is that possible, Lord?) Then I recalled—or it was recalled to me—that I didn't normally extend to them the grace that I knew God was extending to me. In other words, I found myself seeing them more as I believe God sees them—and seeing a few things in myself that God wanted to bring to my attention. Sigh.[17]

Prayer that I hoped might change others ended up changing me. That's one way God chips away at our character to make us more like Jesus. It hurts—but it's also the gospel of change and renewal.

Prayer and God's Purposes for the World

The gospel is not all about me, however, and neither is it all about my relationships, though that is a factor in my personal transformation.

No, God is seeking to put right everything that is presently wrong in the world. As apprentices of Jesus, learning to live the ways of God's kingdom, amazingly enough, we have a part to play in that. It may be through our choice of work, or of where to live, or wherever (please God) we can be agents for gospel-shaped change.

However, that still means we can do nothing about the majority of the world's problems. Except pray for them. I can do that. For pandemics, and refugees, and earthquakes, and the rest of the horrors—for all affected by them and all who seek to help.

Do my prayers make a difference? It would take us too far afield to think about this in depth. Suffice it to say for now that Jesus would lead us to think the answer is yes. Back in the seventeenth century, the first reason the scientist Blaise Pascal gave for "Why God has established prayer" was "To communicate to His creatures the dignity of causality."[18] Praying for the world's problems, and for the good news of God's intervention and grace to be experienced, is not nothing. God allows us to have causality— which, after all, is part of the image of God, the first cause of all things. By some mysterious chemistry that we are not privy to, God weaves those prayers into God's ongoing purposes to redeem the world. Prayer and the gospel are woven inseparably together.

CHAPTER 4

THE GOSPEL AND DISCIPLESHIP

Three More—plus One

My son-in-law is an engineer. One of the things my grandson has learned from him is how to draw two-dimensional plans of three-dimensional objects. One of the first was an exploded drawing of a treehouse he hoped his father would build, complete with numbered parts. The next was a steam train, with separate views of the top, the side, and the front. The grandparents were suitably ecstatic.

In these chapters on discipleship, I am trying to create a two-dimensional representation of a three-dimensional thing—actually four-dimensional, since time is involved too. And that involves treating separately things that in fact belong intrinsically together, like the aspects of that steam train. So far we have touched on three aspects of being an apprentice of Jesus: the fact that it happens in a community of disciples, the fact that our learning is shaped by the redeeming story of Scripture, and the fact that prayer is a key to God's work in us and in the world.

I want now to add four more to that mix. But before I do so, I want to underline that these are not activities in watertight categories. I have separated them for convenience, the convenience of the exploded diagram, but in fact, community, Scripture, and prayer weave in and out of one another, and each is dependent on the others. To be a follower of Jesus, recruited by him to be blessed by his good news and to represent that good news in the world, is a holistic thing. Of course, God may draw attention to one more than the others at particular points in our lives, but ultimately they all converge.

4. COMMUNION: A MEAL TO RENEW DISCIPLES FOR MISSION

Here's an example that's ready to hand: one of the points at which community, Scripture, and prayer come together is the service that different church traditions call Eucharist, Holy Communion, Mass, or the Lord's Supper. And it is my conviction that this service exists to proclaim the gospel and draw us deeper into the mission of God, which is the way the gospel is expressed in practice.

When disciples get together for worship, whether for Communion or not, what exactly are we doing? At the heart of it, we are responding to God's love. We are celebrating the gospel—God's renewing, redeeming, restoring love at work in the world through Jesus Christ. We confess those things in our lives that run counter to this restoring love—our sins. We are reminded that those things can be forgiven and done away with, because that too is part of the good news. We are taught from Scripture more of God's gospel and how it speaks to the world. And we renew our commitment to live as apprentices of Jesus.

When it comes to Communion, however, there is an additional element. Whatever our tradition, the heart of the service is always the same. It is where we remember the most central act from which God's good news flows—the death and resurrection of Jesus. We are reminded that he gave his life for the redemption of the world. But alongside that, we are reminded in a physical way that we are the direct descendants of the disciples at that original supper, who were the first to receive bread and wine from Jesus. How come?

The tradition I know best is the Anglican one, and I have come to appreciate the way it connects God's mission and our discipleship. Forgive me if this is not your way of doing things. You will know better than I how this works out in your own worship.

For Anglicans—and this would be true for most liturgical traditions—in the lead-up to the actual communion, there is a long prayer called the Prayer of Consecration. As a child, I used to find this interminably boring. Now I see its wisdom. Basically, what the Prayer of Consecration does is to locate communion firmly at the heart of the Bible's six-act play. Watch how it works:

- One of these prayers says, "It is indeed right that we should praise you, gracious God, for you created all things [there's act 1 of the play]. . . . When we turned away from you in sin [there's a reference to act 2], you did cease to care for us, but opened a path of salvation for all people." Then "you made a covenant with your people Israel, and through your servants Abraham and Sarah gave the promise of a blessing to all nations [and there's a summary of act 3]."[1]

- The prayer then moves to describe act 4 of the play: how God has intervened in our world in the person of Jesus—his life, death, and resurrection—to put everything right. We say, "In the fullness of time, you sent your Son Jesus Christ, to share our human nature, to live and die as one of us to reconcile us to you."

- Some versions of the prayer (there are several) even look ahead to act 6, the end of the story: "In the fullness of time, reconcile all things in Christ and make them new, and bring us to that city of light where you dwell with all your sons and daughters; through Jesus Christ our Lord, the firstborn of all creation, the Head of the Church and the author of our salvation."

- Then we return to act 4, the reason we are at worship. "On the night he was betrayed, Jesus took bread . . ." And we are reminded of that last meal Jesus shared with his disciples.

This is where we enter the story. I imagine it this way. The bread goes from Jesus to John, who passes it to Peter, who passes it to James, who passes it to Andrew, and so on until it comes to the end of the line—perhaps to Bartholomew. And then Bartholomew turns—and it is not the end of the line after all. Who is next? Guess what: the next disciple in line is you. And I am there too. And so is everyone who receives the bread and the wine. It was disciples who took part in the first communion; it is disciples who take part today. There is a direct and unbroken line of succession from them to us.

As a result, every time we hold out our hands to receive communion, it is Jesus giving us the bread. We are identifying ourselves with the first disciples in the Upper Room and saying, "Yes, Jesus, we are your disciples too. We turn away from the sin that runs counter to your good news. We want your bread and wine, your body and blood, in us. Yes, Jesus, we are committed to you and the work you began by your death and resurrection. We want to be your body broken for the life of the world. Yes, Jesus, we are committed to your mission to renew all things." Act 4 leads seamlessly into act 5, where we are drawn into the story to play our parts in God's mission.

This is why, at the end of the service, act 5 is reinforced: "May we, who share his body, live his risen life; we, who drink his cup, bring life to others; we, whom the Spirit lights, give light to the world."[2] There is the mission, continuing in and through us, Jesus's disciples today. And so we are blessed and sent out with new strength and vision to take part in God's mission to the world.

Billy Graham believed that Christians need two conversions: one from the world to Christ and the other with Christ into the world.[3] And at the hinge between those two movements stands the communion service. It is because of the mission of God calling us to apprenticeship that we come to this service, and it is because of our apprenticeship that we are sent out from this service to continue in the mission of God.

5. OBEDIENCE: DOING WHAT YOU'RE TOLD

The next element in Christian apprenticeship is in many ways the toughest. The word *obedience* has gotten a bad rap in our world: it smacks too much of authoritarianism and someone undermining my personal freedom. One friend suggested I use the phrase "responsive choices," instead of the word *obedience*. I am hoping that the word *obedience* can be redeemed. But maybe I am overly optimistic.

Here's one place to start. The fact is that we are all obedient, perhaps twenty times every day, and we hardly notice it. We obey traffic signals, the directions on a medicine bottle, the rules of language, the call of "Dinner's ready!" or the advice of a personal trainer without a moment's thought. (You could try counting how often you are obedient in a single day. You might be surprised.)

Why do we obey these things, these people? Because—quite simply—we know that obeying in these ways is good for us. This kind of obedience makes life livable, and it's become habitual. It's just part of who we are. We hardly think of these situations as examples of "obedience." We don't often feel that these things cramp our personal freedom: in fact, we know perfectly well that without them, there could be no real freedom. (Obeying a red light, to take just one example, means you keep the freedom to stay alive. It would be foolish to believe that stopping at a red light cramps your freedom.)

Let me put it bluntly: being an apprentice of Jesus means obeying Jesus. He says, "Why do you call me 'Lord, Lord,' and do not do what I tell you?" (Luke 6:46). If Ken had simply gone to class on Mondays, he would never have become an electrician. More importantly, if he hadn't obeyed the directions of the master electrician, he would not be such a fine electrician today. In the same way, we will never be shaped by the values of the kingdom unless we learn that same kind of costly obedience: love your enemies, forgive seventy times seven times, go the second mile, care for the poor, and so on.

Every one of these instructions requires a conscious, deliberate choice to obey—often the opposite of the choice we would naturally make. And it hurts—just like a new exercise at the gym hurts—until it becomes second nature to us. But the ways of the kingdom, which in general are not natural to us, need to become precisely that—*second* nature to us. They are not generally our *first* nature. Dying to that first nature and growing into that second nature is precisely what God's work in our lives is all about.

What does this obedience look like? On one level, it can be quite straightforward. A Catholic missionary in Tanzania told me the following story. A group of Maasai warriors carried a man who had been gored by a wild animal to the local missionary hospital, where the doctor was able to save his life. However, he was curious, since the Maasai would not normally feel responsibility for someone who belonged to another tribe, so he asked the Maasai why they had brought the man to the hospital. The leader replied, "Well, that's the way the story goes." "What do you mean? What story?" asked the doctor. And the elder replied, "I'm not sure I remember it right. But it's something like this: there was this guy who was beaten up by thieves, and people from his own ethnic group kept passing him by. And then someone from a different tribe came by and took care of him. So we knew we had to bring him."[4]

Here is a group of people who have lived a certain way for centuries. Now they hear the gospel, the good news of reconciliation and transformation, and they recognize its goodness—and its challenge—and make a choice to live in a different way, even though it is costly. They put to death the old way of doing things and choose to live in the new way. They have become apprentices, learning the ways of the Teacher.

Of course, the examples in our lives are not always so clearcut. There isn't one particular Bible text to tell us what to do about how to solve the problems of pandemics, or poverty, or space exploration, or genetically modified foods. This is the nature of "faithfully improvising God's story" in act 5. To figure out an authentically Christian response to such issues requires study of lots of parts of the Bible (not just one), much consultation among Christians of different views, trial and error, and lots of prayer. And even then, there may well not be unanimity. But we need to make the effort if we want to be apprentices of Jesus.

This very day, there will inevitably be at least one opportunity for us to obey Jesus—or not. There will be a situation (or two or more) where, if we were not disciples, we might choose to do one thing, but because we are disciples, we will choose to do something else. It may be a time when we can say yes to doing something good.

It may be a time when we have the option of saying no to doing something not so good. It may be that we will have the option to do something that would serve our own interests or would have been destructive to someone else's, and now we have the option of choosing to serve the interests of the kingdom—even when it's costly or embarrassing. Let's pray that we notice that opportunity when it comes and that God gives us strength to obey. It's the way of the gospel—and the way to new life.

6. THE CROSS: THE COST OF DISCIPLESHIP

All three of the Synoptic Gospels record one of the most sobering and even intimidating sentences in the whole Bible: "If any want to become my followers [disciples, students, apprentices], let them deny themselves and take up their cross daily and follow me" (e.g., Luke 9:23).

I was once preaching about the cross at my own church and began by asking the children to count up how many crosses they could see around the sanctuary. The answer was almost a hundred. If you grew up in the church, or perhaps anywhere in the West, you are very familiar with the idea of a cross—perhaps too familiar. But what if I told you that I once met a Roman Catholic priest who had been crucified, not metaphorically but literally? It was done by guerrilla fighters in Vietnam, during the war there in the 1960s. His arms were stretched out and nailed to a tree, and he was expected to die, slowly and in excruciating pain. (There is a reason the words *excruciating* and *crucifixion* come from the same root.)

He did not die, however, and that incident was part of the reason he later became a Christian and then a priest. He told this story to a group of university chaplains sitting around a table in a comfortable old university building, where we were innocently sharing our stories—until that point. When he had finished, our mouths were open. Nobody knew what to say. How could one human being do such a horrendous thing to another? What does it do to you to have been crucified? And to have survived? We did not ask to see his hands and tried not to look. Suddenly, crucifixion was no longer a familiar scene in the Bible—sad, of course, but not gut-wrenching. Now it was something that had happened to David, someone we knew—our friend, our colleague, sitting just a few feet from us. This was different. It was real. And it was horrendous.

When Jesus spoke of taking up your cross, that too was real and horrendous to the first disciples and would-be disciples. They had seen crucifixion. There had been thousands of them. Quite possibly the disciples knew people who had been crucified. The Jewish historian Josephus tells of three friends of his who were crucified.[5] Why would someone choose to pick up a cross? If you did that, there was only one destination possible.

What on earth might Jesus mean? Isn't this the same Jesus who promised "that they may have life, and have it abundantly" (John 10:10)? Why such a cruel and violent image? I believe it is because God's work of renewing all things—ourselves and the world—involves radical surgery. Restoration is not a walk in the park. For example, I don't know about you, but I know for myself how much I cling to my unloving ways, how deep in me is the instinct to put myself before others, how stubbornly I resist doing God's will so I can keep doing what I prefer.

But it will not do. God is relentless. I may not always want God's work in me, but God is determined to do it. This is why we "cannot" be disciples without a cross: the heart of discipleship is death. It is no harsher than saying, "Unless you go to medical school, you cannot be a doctor," or "Unless you train, you will never be an athlete," or even "Unless you breathe, you will die." Those are not mean, sadistic statements. They simply state the way things are. The connection is just as organic and necessary. You want to be an apprentice of Jesus and be turned into a creature who can love fully and freely and who can enter into the dance of the universe? Unless you take up your cross, it's impossible.

To "take up our cross" is thus simply to say yes to the program. That's why the Christian life begins with baptism, a symbol of death.

Does this sound hard? Jesus didn't pull any punches on this subject, and I have no right to try to soften his words. But there is one important thing to balance the harshness, and it is equally biblical: taking up the cross is not an end in itself. Hebrews says bluntly that even Jesus, *"for the sake of the joy that was set before him* endured the cross" (Heb 12:2; italics mine). How did Jesus manage to go through with the crucifixion? One reason is that he knew what lay on the other side, and it gave him courage. What lay on the other side was simply joy.

In C. S. Lewis's *The Screwtape Letters*, the devil Screwtape speaks truth, even though he hates it: "[God] is a hedonist at heart. All those fasts and vigils and stakes and crosses are only a facade. Or only like foam on the sea shore. Out at sea, out in His sea, there is pleasure, and more pleasure. He makes no secret of it; at His right hand are 'pleasures for evermore.'"[6]

I have experienced this death/resurrection sequence, and my guess is that you have too. While I was on the InterVarsity staff at Carleton University in Ottawa in the 1980s, the opportunity came up to speak in a first-year philosophy class. The professor was Marvin Glass, a well-known Marxist atheist, and he always devoted the first part of his freshman class to discussing questions of the meaning of life, the existence of God, the nature of good and evil, and so on. He told me, "I really can't explain to the class in a convincing way why people believe in God, so it's better if you do it." I gulped.

It was one of those occasions when you know God is asking you to do an impossible thing, but you really have to say yes. (It's interesting to reflect on what becomes of freewill in those moments.) After all, I was a disciple of Jesus, and one of the things that marks a disciple is obedience. With fear and trembling, I agreed to do it.

I remember vividly walking to the class on the appointed day and saying to Steve, my colleague who was coming to give me moral and prayer support, "I feel like a condemned man going to his execution." It really felt that bad. As things turned out, the class went pretty well. (These days, I would be far less intimidated by a freshman class.) Discussion went well. And Marvin graciously said nothing. He did point out that he would have the rest of the term to deconstruct what I had said. Fair enough. And he and I had several public debates on the existence of God in the years that followed.

What was really interesting to me about this incident, however, was my spontaneous comment to Steve as we walked away from the class. Without thinking about it, I said, "Wow, I feel alive again, as though I've just had a death sentence lifted and got a new lease on life." As soon as the words were out of my mouth, however, I thought, "Hah! Death and resurrection. Death and resurrection. But of course! That's the kind of thing Jesus was talking about."

The challenge of the cross is not often as painfully obvious as that. More often it is in the little things: choosing to set aside our pride and apologize, giving time to greet the panhandler, giving more to a disaster relief fund than we are comfortable with. These are all examples of laying down our lives, even when we are unaware that's what we are doing. I suspect it is overly optimistic to think that the way of the cross ever becomes a habit for apprentices of Jesus as it was for Jesus himself—but that is God's goal for us.

These, then, are some of the basic elements of discipleship—community, Scripture, prayer, communion, obedience, and the cross. But there is one more—and it is somewhat different.

THE SPIRIT OF JESUS: THE INVISIBLE HELPER

William Temple, once archbishop of Canterbury, said something like this: "It's no good giving me a play like *Hamlet* or *King Lear* and telling me to write a play like that. Shakespeare could do it; I can't. And it is no good showing me a life like the life of Jesus and telling me to live a life like that. Jesus could do it; I can't. But if the genius of Shakespeare could come and live in me, then I could write plays like his. And if the Spirit of Jesus could come and live in me, then I could live a life like his."[7]

The work of shaping us in the life of the kingdom is not something we can achieve by ourselves. Indeed, it's not something we would naturally be interested in—it is so counterintuitive and so demanding. The idea that we should be apprentices in the kingdom is God's idea, conceived in love and mercy. And though Jesus is not present to train us as he did the first twelve, he is still present by his Spirit to do that same work, to enter our experience, to work within our personality, and to make possible a way of living that we would have thought impossible before. This is part of the good news: God is not only promising to renew all things; he is also taking personal responsibility for ensuring it happens.

In fact, it is because of the working of the Spirit of Jesus that those six elements of our apprenticeship can happen:

- It's the Spirit of Jesus working in us who creates Christian community so that we can work and worship and play with people of all backgrounds and races.

- It's that Spirit who helps us understand the Bible and figure out what to do about the things we read.

- It's that Spirit who encourages us to open our lives to Jesus through prayer.

- It's that Spirit who strengthens our apprenticeship in the communion service.

- It's that Spirit who gives us strength of will and creativity to carry out our assignments, to lay down our lives inch by inch.

- And it is that same Spirit who gives us the courage to take up our cross—and who brings resurrection out of death.

In this chapter, we have gotten involved in some of the daily nitty-gritty ways the gospel works like yeast in and through the life of disciples. Now I want to pull the camera back from this close-up view and look instead through a wide-angle lens at the context where all this happens, that thing we call the church.[8]

CHAPTER 5

THE GOSPEL AND THE CHURCH
Back to Basics

It is not news to anyone that many old churches are dying. A few years back, researcher Thom Rainer wrote, "Any guess to the number of closings in 2013 is speculation on my part. I wouldn't be surprised, however, if the numbers reach the 8,000 to 10,000 level."[1] In the United Kingdom, 1,552 churches closed between 2008 and 2013.[2] And of course, the COVID-19 pandemic accelerated that process for many smaller, aging churches.

Yet this is not cause for despair. As many churches come to the end of their lives, many others are just starting out. A friend of mine says churches are like people: every day, some die and others are born. This shouldn't surprise us.

The same UK research reveals that 2,951 churches opened in that same period of 2008 to 2013. But often these new churches take different and unfamiliar forms. They meet in odd places and at odd times, they may or may not have liturgy, they may or may not have ordained leaders, and they may or may not be affiliated with a denomination.[3] So are they really churches? As we look to the future, we need some answers.

Perhaps we can think of it this way. When the human body is in danger, the blood concentrates on protecting the essential organs, and the peripheral parts (fingers, toes, ears) may suffer. That's why we faint (in the heat) or get frostbite (in the cold). In the same way, in the church's present crisis, it is important to know what the "essential organs" of the church are—and maybe to let some of the others go for the sake of survival.

The example of the Kodak company is well known. It seems to have been Thom Schultz of Group Publishing who first noticed the parallel between the company and the church.[4] For once, it seems adequate to quote Wikipedia:

> During most of the 20th century Kodak held a dominant position in photographic film, and in 1976, had an 89% market share of photographic film sales in the United States. The company's ubiquity was such that its tagline "Kodak moment" entered the common lexicon to describe a personal event that demanded to be recorded for posterity.
>
> Kodak began to struggle financially in the late 1990s as a result of the decline in sales of photographic film and its slowness in transitioning to digital photography, despite having invented the core technology used in current digital cameras.[5]

In January 2012, Kodak filed for Chapter 11 bankruptcy protection in the United States District Court for the Southern District of New York.

An article in the *Harvard Business Review* suggests why the company ran into trouble. The author, Scott Anthony, submits that Kodak failed to ask, "What business are we in today? . . . Define the problem you are solving for customers, or, in our parlance 'the job you are doing for them.' For Kodak, that's the difference between framing itself as a chemical film company vs. an imaging company vs. a moment-sharing company."[6]

Anthony suggests that what Kodak was best at was fulfilling its slogan of "share memories, share life." Ironically, they acquired a photo-sharing site called Ofoto in 2001. I say "ironically" because that was three years before Facebook began. If Kodak had positioned Ofoto differently, it could have filled the same role as Facebook, helping people "share memories, share life," but it didn't. Instead, "Kodak used Ofoto to try to get more people to print digital images"—that is, to bolster its traditional business. Needless to say, it didn't work.[7]

The question for a declining church, therefore, is not "How can we get back to business as it was fifty years ago?" or even "What can we do to get new people into the pews?" I recently heard of one minister who said, "I think if I keep tweaking Sunday morning, eventually people will come back." But tweaking Sunday morning is not going to help. The fundamental question is "What business is the church in? What are we really about?"[8]

I would argue that every church in every age and every culture begins with the gospel—the good news about God that Jesus announced. As we have seen, this leads directly to the invitation for men and women to "repent and believe," to be baptized, and to become Jesus's apprentices in the trade school of the kingdom—also known as the church. At its heart, therefore, the church is people who have responded to the gospel of Jesus. It is, if you like, the place where gospel people gather, a gospel-shaped community. Nothing more, nothing less.

Having said "nothing more," of course, there are many other things that mark the life of churches. What about the structural things: the liturgies and committees and budgets, the orders of service and websites and music groups? What about pastors and bishops and presbyteries, councils and synods and annual reports? They loom large in the life of most churches and denominations and in the way the church is perceived in the world at large. How do they fit with this image of church as filled with gospel people?

Think of it this way. The gospel is water—pure, clear, refreshing water; indeed, it is the water of life, life for the world. And it is important that the water remain pure—H_2O. There are other compounds whose components sound very similar: H_3O (hydronium), H_2O_2 (hydrogen peroxide), Ho (holmium), and so on. But none is a substitute for H_2O, and some of those things would be very bad for you. Hence Paul's strong reaction against those who "want to pervert the gospel of Christ" (Gal 1:7). Of course he's upset: they are trying to sell contaminated water to thirsty people.

And the church is the guardian, the steward, of that precious water, to make it available to the world. So what should we keep the water in? And how can we make it available to those who need it?

- One Christian says, "All my life I've drunk the water from the best cut-glass wineglasses. To me, that represents the preciousness of the water and links us to the generations who drank from those same glasses before us. That's really the only suitable way to keep the water."

- Then someone else responds, "But I need the water while I'm driving around, and I really can't carry an expensive wineglass around in my car. It's asking for trouble. Why can't I carry the water in a travel mug?"

- Perhaps a third person only has a cheap plastic tumbler from a convenience store. Will that do for carrying the water? Well, actually it will, even though it is far from aesthetically pleasing and hardly conveys a sense of tradition.

- And finally, if you were stuck out in a hot desert with nothing to drink and someone offered you water in a flower vase, would you drink it? I suspect you would. Not under normal circumstances, of course, but these are not normal circumstances.

You can probably think of other water containers and when they might be appropriate, but you see my point. What is important is the water, not so much the container. We have our personal preference for one container rather than another depending on our context and our taste and our tradition, but the important thing is that the water be available to those who need it—and to us.

Having said that, of course, there are some obvious requirements for any water container, whatever materials it is made of—glass, metal, or plastic:

- A good container has to be reasonably rigid. It's tricky to drink from a water balloon.

- A good container mustn't be contaminated with anything else. For example, it can't contain a chemical that will dissolve and leach into the water. Otherwise the water will be something other than H_2O.

- A good container can't be totally enclosed. There has to be an opening, and it is generally at the top, not the bottom—unless there is a tap on it.

But those requirements still leave lots of room for variety.

Here's a real-life example of gospel water in a container that is at the same time familiar and unfamiliar. In 2006, I visited Tanzania and had breakfast one day with a Roman Catholic priest, Pat Patten, who had been involved in the creation of a Maasai church back in the 1970s. Here is how he described the Eucharist as it was practiced among the Maasai at that time:

> We would start in the evening when the cows were coming in and the elders would gather up green grass. Green grass is a really powerful symbol of forgiveness, and anyone holding green grass, is saying, I'm OK with everybody around here. And if I'm not, I have to go to the person I'm not OK with and get things right.
>
> And so, as the cows were coming in the evening, people would gather the green grass and then, when the cows were milked and everybody was full and at ease, there's a traditional song the women and men sing. They go in concentric circles, counter rotating, singing two different songs that blend fabulously. And then each woman brings a new piece of firewood. All the fires in the households are extinguished, and the warriors start a brand-new fire by rubbing fire sticks together.
>
> And then people would start discussing in the group from the circle what [Bible] story most touched them. And there would be some discussion and then kind of a consensus. And then someone would tell the gospel story and they would tell what happened [in their lives]. And it was not always a success story, it would be sometimes, you know, "We should have been able to do this better," or "It worked partway."
>
> That would be finished then with a communion service, which was done on a cow skin, on which all of their special

ceremonies are done, with the *olorika*, the three-legged stool there, and a gourd filled with wine, and a half buffalo horn (they are sliced longitudinally and resemble an artistically shaped plate) with bread on it and everyone would be signed with chalk in the form of a cross on their foreheads. For the Maasai, chalk is a sacred symbol of new birth, of initiation, of new beginnings, and in the evening in the firelight, you would see this vivid white on these black faces.

And then people would share the gourd and the buffalo horn and there would be interspersed the Maasai songs. I don't know if you've heard the chant—they always kind of chant—there is always a verse and a refrain. Someone will lead and sing a verse and then everybody sings the response. And it's a quick back and forth interaction in the singing, not longer drawn out verses, the way we often have.

And then in the end, one of the people from the oldest age groups would stand up and take the fresh milk from the cow and gather up all the grass, put it in the gourd, and then sprinkle everybody heavily with milk as a sign of blessing. And then the women would each take a piece of wood from the new fire and take it back to their homes.

Then we would stay there the night and leave in the morning.[9]

I have often had discussions with church groups about this story. What is familiar here? What are the things that we recognize as characteristic of church as we understand it? Or to put it another way, in what ways is this a good container for the gospel water? And then, on the other hand, what seems strange to us?

Christians in the West resonate with a few things in this story:

- the need for reconciliation before coming to the table
- the serious interaction with Scripture (How did we do in obeying Jesus this week?)
- the centrality of bread and wine in the service
- singing in worship

These are clearly apprentices of Jesus, involved in worshipping and learning to obey him—perhaps with more seriousness than many of us in the West. I get the feeling that a Maasai who knew nothing of Christian faith would soon pick up what the gospel is all about in that context. We recognize, almost intuitively, that this is church. It is a gospel-shaped community.

But then there are more aspects of this service that are unfamiliar to Western culture:

- fresh grass as a symbol of reconciliation[10]

- the degree to which reconciliation is taken seriously (This is not just a perfunctory "passing of the peace" or "take a moment to greet your neighbor.")

- gathering in the open air around a fire

- the extinguishing and (later) relighting of the home fires

- the dancing and the nature of the singing

- the cow skin as communion table, the three-legged stool, the gourd, and the buffalo horn

- the chalk crosses on the foreheads of the worshippers

- sprinkling with milk

This seems to me a lovely illustration of the simple but crucial fact that "church" looks different in different places and at different times. At the same time, there are things that all churches have in common—they may not be many in number, but they are recognizable and each one is hugely significant. The water remains the same though the container is different.

Changes in culture always press church leaders and theologians to revisit this question of what is primary (and essential) to the church and what is secondary (and can be changed). In the Protestant Reformation of the sixteenth century, for example, the Roman Catholic understanding of church was being widely challenged. Christopher Schoon summarizes this as an attempt "to shift the Church's identity from the hierarchical strata of clergy, cathedrals, and basilicas into more accessible practices that would benefit the people gathering in the local churches."[11] In other words, putting the living water within reach of those who needed it.

This would explain the Reformed view of the church that many Protestant churches have inherited, often unknowingly. What was that view? John Calvin summarized the majority opinion: "Wherever we see the Word of God purely preached and listened to, and the sacraments administered according to the institution of Christ, we must not doubt that there is a Church."[12] So word and sacrament. There is the irreducible minimum. If those things are in place, you have a church, and everything else can be built on those foundations.[13]

Now the culture has shifted again, and that definition seems inadequate. South African missiologist David Bosch points out some of the limitations of the Reformation view when applied to our present context:

- "The church was defined in terms of what happens inside its four walls, not in terms of its calling to the world."

- The verbs are passive (the gospel is taught, the sacraments are administered): "It is a place where something is done, not a living organism doing something."

- Despite the emphasis on correct theology, "the church of pure doctrine was . . . a church without mission, and its theology more scholastic than apostolic."[14]

- We could add that in the Reformation model, everything depends on the pastor/teacher, who is responsible for Word, sacrament, and discipline. There is little sense of ministry as the work of the body of Christ.

As a result, many are saying it is time to revisit the question, What exactly is church? This is not just a trendy thing to do, arising out of a sense of our own superiority to previous generations of Christians. ("They said X, but now of course we know better."[15]) The need is much more fundamental than that.

The Reformation's reformulation was not just an academic exercise. The Reformers saw how the understanding of the church had become calcified over the centuries and was holding the church back from being all that Christ had called it to be. The point of redefining the church was to strip it of the barnacles of tradition and to streamline it for renewed vitality. The point of seeking a fresh understanding of church today is the same. Behind it lies the question, How can the church in our generation be a more culturally appropriate container for the water of the gospel? Here are a couple of attempts to do so.

GEORGE LINGS

British missiologist George Lings suggests that there need to be four dimensions for "church" to be a suitable container for the water of life—*up*, *in*, *out*, and *of*:[16]

UP: WORSHIP
Church begins with God, just as (by the same token) the gospel begins with God. A Christian community will therefore center on God and the worship of God in Jesus Christ.

IN: COMMUNITY
Jesus's apprentices are a community—the New Testament calls it his body, his family, his temple, his army.[17] These are wildly diverse images, but they have some things in common. In each one there is diversity. In each one there is a close unity, and in each one there is mutual dependence. In the Christian community, the members can be—you may have noticed—wildly different, but they need to be united, and they need to support one another and be supported by one another. That's how we experience the gospel; that's how we extend the kingdom.

OUT: MISSION
The reason church exists at all is because of the mission of God, into which the gospel is a window. When Jesus explains the gospel, we hear about the mission. When we are baptized, we join the mission. Thus a central reason the

church exists is to be a junior partner in the work of God in the world.

OF: CONNECTION

The meaning of "the body of Christ" is ambivalent: it is at the same time the local body of believers and the universal body of Christ.[18] Both are important in the mission of God. Thus a local church cannot afford to "go it alone" in mission. "Independent church" is a theological oxymoron.[19] Whether the connection is formal (through a denomination) or informal (through a fellowship of ministers) is secondary, but there needs to be one.

Then Lings makes a very smart move. He points out that these four dimensions bear a close resemblance to the marks of the church listed in the Nicene Creed: "one, holy, catholic and apostolic." "One" speaks of community. "Holy" speaks of our relationship with God, focused in worship. "Catholic" or "universal" refers to our connection with other churches. And "apostolic" reminds us of our mission. (See figure 5.1.)

Of course, theology always emerges from a cultural context; it does not come down from heaven as an eternal absolute. So it is helpful to know that Lings is writing in an English context where there are many experimental forms of church, and he is trying to find a minimal definition of church that will help the acceptance of these fresh expressions of church. What is brilliant about what he does here is that he ties these new communities in to the definition of church found in the historic creeds, thus giving fresh expressions of church the credibility they are often assumed to lack.

For such new, nontraditional churches, his definition is very helpful. I was speaking recently to a church planter whose denomination is not quite sure whether the new church she started is "really" a church in the traditional sense. It meets not in a dedicated church building but in a restaurant. Many of the members don't have a lot of money, so it's unlikely that the church will ever be financially self-supporting or pay its dues to the denomination's head office. One can understand the denomination's hesitancy.

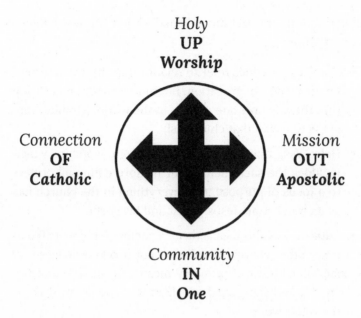

Holy
UP
Worship

Connection   *Mission*
OF   **OUT**
Catholic   **Apostolic**

Community
IN
One

FIGURE 5.1. The four dimensions of church[20]

I asked four questions, based on George Lings's outline:

- Does this new community worship together, including celebrating communion together?
- Do they feel themselves to be a community where people care for one another?
- Do they have a sense of mission and of serving the community in which they exist?
- Do they connect in a cooperative kind of way with other churches?

The answer to all four was a resounding yes. (It is worth adding that the links to other churches are more within the city and across denominations than within the "official" denomination.) To my mind, that's church: one, holy, catholic, and apostolic.

It is worth adding that there has never been a formal, universally accepted definition of these four terms. However, they are generally understood more broadly than the way Lings works with them. Thus:

- *One*: Yes, this does refer to relationships between believers in a local congregation. But more broadly, it is saying that there is only one church in the world. (Opinion varies as to which that church is!)

- *Holy*: Yes, this is expressed through worship—which includes the sacraments—but it more commonly refers to a focus of purpose, that everything in the church has as its touchstone Jesus Christ and his gospel.

- *Catholic*: Yes, this means that every church is connected to every other church, whether or not it acknowledges that fact. But the word primarily means "universal"—that the church and the gospel of which it is the steward is for the whole world.

- *Apostolic*: Yes, it means involved in the mission of God, in that *apostolic* means "having been sent." But more traditionally, apostolic means standing in line of descent from the first disciples and their teaching, handed down to us in Scripture. Having said that, it seems to me that in this case, Lings is recalling us to another aspect of "apostolic," that of being sent in mission, one that is all too often forgotten in our churches. We need this reminder.

What Lings does, however, is what missiologists are always required to do—indeed, what any theologian ought to do—to exercise faithful improvisation, honoring the tradition while rethinking it for a fresh context. And, amid our present realities, what he has done here seems to me a very helpful move.

So there is one attempt to identify the core marks of the church—the essentials of a gospel container. Here is another attempt, this time not theological in approach but historical.

ANDREW WALLS

Christianity Today once described Andrew Walls as "the most important person you don't know."[21] That's a shrewd assessment. Walls has had a huge influence on thinking about the church's mission for decades, but it has been largely behind the scenes. His books are few but dense with insights and thought-provoking stories. Here's one of those stories.

Walls asks us to imagine an interplanetary professor of comparative religions from another planet who visits earth at intervals of several centuries to try to understand this thing called "church":[22]

- First, he visits a group of Jewish believers in Jerusalem a few years after the time of Jesus. They look largely like other Jewish folk of that time. They worship in the temple, take part in animal sacrifice, and observe the Sabbath. They have a strong sense of family and are devoted to the Scriptures. What makes them distinctive, however, is their belief that Jesus was and is the Messiah, the Son of Man, and the Suffering Servant foretold in their Scriptures who would usher in the world's last days.

- The professor's next stop is in the year 325 CE, when he visits the council where the Nicene Creed is being hammered out. He discovers some differences from his first visit. These people are not Jewish. If anything, they are somewhat hostile to Jews. Clergy are not married. They are horrified at the idea of animal sacrifice. And if a Christian baby were to be circumcised, the parents would be regarded as having abandoned their faith. They revere the same holy book as the Jerusalem Christians but treat more recent documents with equal reverence. Their concern right now is to find the precisely correct terminology to describe the relationship between God the Father and God the Son.

- The third visit takes our professor to Scotland in the sixth century, where he observes Celtic monks. Some are standing in ice-cold water with their arms outstretched, praying the Psalms. One is being beaten for having failed to say "Amen" to the prayer of thanks before a meal. Some are sailing off in a little boat, bearing beautiful manuscripts, to evangelize some of the Scottish tribes.

- On his next visit, the scholar visits England in the nineteenth century, where a group of smartly dressed evangelical ladies and gentlemen in London are discussing the evangelization of the heathen in Africa, some six thousand miles away. They are also passing motions to try to abolish slavery. Many of them carry Bibles containing the same documents that each of the previous groups had valued.

- Finally, the professor, now thoroughly confused, visits an Indigenous church in Lagos, Nigeria. There, the people are processing through the streets, claiming to be Cherubim and Seraphim, proclaiming the power of God to speak and to heal. They too rely on the Bible and agree with the Nicene Creed . . . though the latter doesn't greatly interest them.

The challenge for the scholar trying to figure out what church is, of course, is to discern what—if anything—these groups have in common. He finally pinpoints four things:

1. Each group focuses on Jesus.

2. All use the same Scriptures (though it is true that the first group have no "New Testament").

3. Although there are some differences, each group practices baptism and communion.

4. All see themselves as being in continuity with the people of Israel in the Old Testament.

The one thing that Lings stresses but Walls does not is mission. So was mission a priority in the historical examples Walls gives?

- The first years of the Christian faith certainly saw remarkably rapid growth, both within and beyond the Jewish community.

- The century that saw the formulation of the Nicene Creed also saw Christianity become the formal religion of the Roman Empire and spread to Armenia, "the first independent ethnic nation to become Christian," and to parts of Africa, such as Ethiopia and Nubia.[23]

- The monks of the sixth century were passionate in their spreading of the gospel, whatever the cost. Missiologist Dana Robert says that "monks were the grassroots missionaries in the conversion of Europe."[24] Among other achievements, forty monks arrived to evangelize England in the late sixth century, and "on Christmas Day 597, priests baptized the king and 10,000 English warriors."[25]

- The nineteenth-century evangelicals in his illustration are very concerned for mission as they understood it and took the gospel (and often, it has to be admitted, British culture as well) to the corners of the British Empire.

- The contemporary Nigerian Christians are certainly confident in their public witness and their promise of healing, and the church across Africa continues to grow at an unprecedented speed.

So although Walls doesn't highlight it, in fact all five of his groups, in spite of their wild diversity, were marked by a commitment to mission.

THE GOSPEL CORE

Maybe you prefer one of these scholars' definitions over the other. Or maybe you have your own. In one way it doesn't matter. The basic question always has to be, Can we trace the influence of the gospel in the way these communities are shaped? Can we discern the outline of the gospel in the way they live? There will always be cultural differences. But we can always ask, Is Jesus and his transforming work at the heart of these groups?

Let me try to show what happens when you apply the question to the definitions of the church offered by Lings and Walls. Take Lings's list first:

- *One*: We try to be united. Why? Because the gospel calls us to unity as the Trinity is united. Unity is a fruit of the gospel.

- *Holy*: We engage in worship because Christ by his death and resurrection has opened the way for us to do so. Not to mention that God as seen in the gospel is amazing and worthy of worship!

- *Catholic*: We have a bond with Christians of every tradition and every culture because we have all tasted the gospel and are engaged in the same gospel work.

- *Apostolic*: The gospel of God's mission through Jesus energizes the core of our lives.

What then of Walls's list? The same is true:

- A focus on *Jesus*: Of course—Jesus is himself the gospel.

- A focus on *the Bible*: The story of God's good news over time.

- A focus on the *sacraments*: Both baptism and communion speak of the gospel and our response to it.

- A focus on *continuity with Israel*: The Old Testament is the story of God's people responding to God's renewing grace—"the gospel beforehand."

So yes, the good news of Jesus is at the heart of both these definitions of the church. Where there is no gospel, there can be no true church. Of course, that gospel will be expressed in different ways in different times and places—which is why discernment is so crucial and often difficult—but that is the key.

FIRST THINGS FIRST

I started with the image of essential organs in the human body. If we unpacked that image further, it would take us back to Paul's picture of the church as a body,[26] with Christ being its head,

Christ who personifies the good news. Without that—without him—we are nothing.

I know it's possible to push an image too far, but maybe we could stretch this one just one stage further—and then I promise to stop. Let's say then that the marks of the church identified by George Lings and Andrew Walls are the essential organs of the church.

But then the other things—the arms and legs, the nerves, and the muscles, directed by the head, empowered by the heart, enabled by the essential organs—are what enables the body to function normally.

So what of those other things—the structural things that mark the life of the church week in and week out? Things like planning the online service, maintaining the building, meeting the budget, working on committees, arranging for pastoral care, and so on? The list is endless, but you get the idea. You have been there and done that many times (perhaps too many times).

Are those not important? Can we just dispense with them? Of course not. Things would fall apart very quickly. We will be talking about church and its structures more in later chapters, so I will just say this for the time being. Here is a metaphor that helps me think about this. Suppose you were to go into an artist's studio. At first it might appear totally chaotic: scattered around the room you would find easels and canvases, palettes and tubes of paint, and lots of brushes, jars of water, aprons, and rags for wiping your hands on. But all these things are in the service of the work of art that is slowly coming into existence on an easel in the corner. And when that is finished and on display in an art gallery, there will be none of the paraphernalia that enables it to come into existence.

As Stephen Covey said, "The main thing is to keep the main thing the main thing."[27] The danger for every church—indeed, every Christian—is that the functional things (like the arguments over the price of the new carpet in the lounge) become the be-all and end-all of church life. Jesus once warned his hearers, "Remember Lot's wife." She looked back when she should have been moving forward and as a result was turned into a pillar of salt.[28] In our present context, the cultural equivalent might be "Remember Kodak."

Until we remember who we are, we cannot invite others to join. But if we are clear about our identity as followers of Jesus, we have a wonderful reality to offer to the world. Exactly how we offer it will be the subject of the next chapter.

CHAPTER 6

THE GOSPEL AND EVANGELISM

Can It Be Redeemed?

So far, I have suggested three things:

1. The heart of Christian faith is not religion, nor morality, nor even the hope of life after death but the good news that God is at work in the world through Jesus Christ to right all wrongs.

2. A Christian is someone who has said yes to Jesus's call to apprenticeship and to learn from him what it means to play our part in this new thing God is doing.

3. The church is the community of Jesus's followers, gathering to worship and learn from him and scattering to live his healing love in the world.

If you are with me thus far, you may find the topic of this chapter jarring and even unnerving. "What?" you may ask. "I like what you have said about living out the love of God in the world. But why do you have to try to drag evangelism out of the red-light district of the church onto Main Street?[1] Why can't you leave it where it was?"

My quick answer is that evangelism is an intrinsic part of being a disciple of Jesus. It is one of the items on Jesus's curriculum for students in his school. I suspect I'm going to have to convince you that is right, so let's begin.

What exactly is evangelism? The heart of evangelism is talking about the gospel. And one reason it is important is that words are important, and verbal communication is important.

In early 2016, a photograph circulated on the internet of a group of young people in the Rijksmuseum in Amsterdam. They were sitting in front of one of the museum's most famous paintings, *The Night Watch* by Rembrandt. Yet not one of them was looking at the picture. Instead, they were all bent over, looking at their phones. You can imagine the internet's reaction. Comments circulated on Twitter such as "The 'distracted' society. No wonder we're in the shape we're in now. Teach your children!" and "What a sad picture of today's society!" However, the true explanation was this: "The students were in fact attentive to the art works, using the museum's freely downloadable multimedia tour."[2] Far from being distracted, they were actually learning about the history, the provenance, and the techniques of the painting they had just been looking at.

We say, "One picture is worth a thousand words." For Christians, however, it is equally true—and sometimes more so—that "sometimes a picture needs a thousand words."[3] The story of the young people in the Rijksmuseum is sad, but the consequences of misinterpreting a picture can be much more serious than that. One of my teachers, James I. Packer, highlights this: "Whoever could have *guessed*, without being told, that the man Jesus was God incarnate, that he had created the world in which he was crucified [and] that by dying a criminal's death he put away the sins of mankind?"[4]

If we had been first-century Jews, passing by the scene of the crucifixion, what might we have thought? "Ah, how sad. Those Romans are such brutes. I wonder if he was really a criminal, or another failed messiah, or just someone who got on the wrong side of the Romans?" And then we would have gone on with our lives. But to know truly what was going on, we would have needed someone to talk to us and give us the true explanation.

This is why I say that evangelism means talking. Talking about Christian faith. Talking about how the gospel is good news. Talking about Jesus. And yes, I am aware that that makes many of us uncomfortable. However, talking is an inescapable part of the story.

Jesus talked about the good news of the kingdom. He talked about it, then he demonstrated it, then he talked about it some more. He called disciples to be his apprentices, to hang out with him and learn to do the kind of things he did—one of which was talking about and explaining the kingdom. It's right there in the story.

So far, so good. But then, at the end of Matthew's Gospel, Jesus gives what is often called the Great Commission, his "famous last words" to the disciples: "All authority in heaven and on earth has been given to me. Go therefore and make disciples of all nations, baptizing them in the name of the Father and of the Son and of the Holy Spirit, and teaching them to obey everything that I have commanded you. And remember, I am with you always, to the end of the age" (Matt 28:16–20).

You may wish to tell me that there is nothing here about evangelism, or even about the gospel. But this doesn't let us off the hook. The core is "make disciples." Many commentators have pointed out that there is only one command, one imperative, in this commission: "make disciples."[5] The other verbs—"go," "baptizing," and "teaching"—revolve around that center. Even "go" in the Greek is actually "going"—in other words, "as you go"—which emphasizes that Jesus's point is not so much the going as the making of disciples. (See figure 6.1.)

To be a Christian is to cooperate with Jesus in the work of God's kingdom. Now he makes it clear that part of that work is helping other people become apprentices of Jesus too. How do we do that? Well, how did Jesus do it? We've seen him do it already.

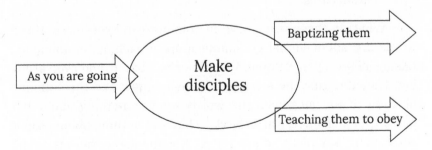

FIGURE 6.1. Make disciples

Three things: he talked about the kingdom, he demonstrated what it was like by the way he lived, and he invited people to be a part of it. And guess what: the first and the third are to do with talking.

Why single out talking when it's so difficult and uncomfortable? Isn't "evangelism" a broader thing than that? Certainly it is true that many things apart from talking are involved in people becoming disciples. More on that later. But the word *evangelism* itself refers to the talking part of that process. How come? It has always been sobering for me as a professor of evangelism to realize that the word *evangelism* never occurs in the New Testament. In fact, the word was not coined until the sixteenth century, and the first reference to it is in the writings not of a theologian, and certainly not of an evangelist, but of Francis Bacon, one of the inventors of the scientific method—which should alert us to its limitations.[6] If you think about it, an "-ism" is generally an abstract thing, a subject for academic study—and the Bible has little time for such things.

Instead, the New Testament uses three related words, none of them particularly abstract:

- *The evangel*: This is the Greek word meaning "the good news of God." You may notice that it contains the word *angel*, meaning "a messenger."

- *To evangelize*: The activity of telling that good news. In fact, you could translate this word as "good newsing." In the Old Testament, the word is generally used of a messenger bringing news of a military victory.

- *An evangelist*: A person who speaks the *evangel* and thus evangelizes.[7]

What do these three have in common? In every case, these words are about verbal communication: preaching, announcing, talking, chatting, explaining, sometimes reasoning, and even arguing. They describe the message, the messenger, and the communication of the message. The words suggest nothing about the messenger's character or lifestyle. They say nothing about "silent witness" or "a ministry of presence," though I agree there is a time for these. No, evangelism is talking. As Walter Brueggemann puts it,

"At the center of the act of evangelism is the message announced, a verbal, out-loud assertion of something decisive not known until this moment of utterance."[8] Evangelism is passing on information that someone does not yet have. It is telling people things they do not know.

Now, at this point you are probably itching to quote Francis of Assisi to me. "Ah," you will say, "but didn't Saint Francis say, 'Preach the gospel at all times. If necessary, use words'?" Very witty. Everyone smiles when they hear this. Many nod, often with relief. But actually, no, he didn't say it. At least, according to historians, it's 99 percent certain he didn't. It's as unlikely and incongruous as if Jesus had urged his followers, "Follow your dreams." For one thing, the first reference to the saying comes from three hundred years after Francis's time, which should make us suspicious. But then even more significantly, in his lifetime, Francis was known as a preacher, and he trained his followers to preach too.[9]

Having said that, I readily admit that the quotation does make an important point: Christlike actions are crucial to communicating the gospel. In fact, the reason people took Jesus's verbal message seriously was that they had seen the truth of what he said in his actions. His words explained the reality of his life. However, right now, I'm just saying that's not what evangelism is—and Francis didn't believe it was evangelism either. Words and actions do not communicate in the same way, and it's not helpful to equate them. Evangelism means talking: opening your mouth and saying something. As in the story of the Rijksmuseum—and the story of the cross—words are essential. As Ed Stetzer has said, "Using that statement [attributed to Francis] is a bit like saying, 'Feed the hungry at all times. If necessary, use food.'"[10]

MY (WORKING) DEFINITION(S)

Over the years that I was a professor of evangelism, I developed a definition of evangelism. But from time to time, it changed. Looking back through my files, I see the original version was

Evangelism is helping people take steps toward faith in Jesus.

Then I realized that "faith" was an unhelpful word, since it is so widely misunderstood. (Mark Twain said, "Faith is believing what you know ain't so." That's a fairly common understanding.) I then changed "faith" to "being disciples of Jesus," since that gives "faith" some specific Christian content. Then for reasons you have heard already, "disciples" turned into "apprentices." Then I realized I had not given space to the Holy Spirit. By this time, it was getting somewhat longer:

> Evangelism is cooperating with the Holy Spirit to help people take steps toward being apprentices of Jesus.

Next, I had the epiphany that evangelism is about talking. (Why did I not realize it sooner?) So the definition became

> Evangelism is cooperating with the Holy Spirit to speak words that help people take steps toward being apprentices of Jesus.

Of course, it won't have escaped your notice that what the definition gains in precision it loses in memorability. That's the way these things go.

But there is a snag with this. If part of the church's responsibility is to make new disciples, that normally requires much more than words,[11] even though the words are crucial. What to do? I ended up with a broad definition and a narrow definition. The narrow one is the one that stresses words. The broad one simply says,

> Evangelism is cooperating with the Holy Spirit to help people take steps toward being apprentices of Jesus.

Am I trying to have my cake and eat it? Well, that's always nice if you can find a way to do it. Maybe the way to have both in this case is to put it like this: all sorts of things help people become disciples (as we'll see), but at some point, words have to be spoken and something has to be said out loud about Jesus.

Let's look more closely at the broad definition. In the first place, it reminds us that evangelism is not really our work: it is the Holy Spirit who is the *agent* in people becoming disciples of Jesus. That should take some pressure off us, since it means it's not all dependent on us. The Spirit of Jesus wants thirsty people to experience the living water of the gospel more than we do. But it's still pretty challenging, since it means we have to make ourselves available to the Holy Spirit—and God only knows where that might lead us.

I also wanted in this definition to make clear the *goal* of evangelism. It's not about making people religious, or getting them to make a "decision for Christ," or persuading them to attend our church. In the first place, it's for them to become followers, disciples—apprentices—of Jesus. That's what human beings were made for. It's not always easy, as you know well if you've been a Christian for more than about a week, but it is ultimately the road to joy.

One practical thing in this definition is the *means* by which evangelism happens. It's a process of "taking steps." There may be very many of those steps, and the process often takes a long time. People who become Christians as adults say it often took months or even years for them to come to the point of becoming disciples. A friend of mine was baptized recently and said, "After ten years of thinking about it, I decided it was time!"[12]

So what can the church do? We can *help*. That help can take many forms. Actions, relationships, experiences, and (don't forget) at some point words all contribute to that process. But all those things can do is help. They cannot accomplish a person's coming to faith by themselves.

I remember speaking about this in Kenya once. For some reason, when I was explaining the bit about "helping," I added "like a midwife" to my explanation. Immediately, a woman in the front row began smiling broadly and nodding vigorously. There are times when a preacher knows he has to stop and invite interaction. This was one of them. I stopped and asked, "You're not a midwife by any chance, are you?"

"Indeed, I am," she replied.

"So tell us what exactly you do," I said.

"Well," she said, "my job is to help the mother and to help the baby. In a way, I'm a servant to both of them. I have to help the mother do what she has to do and help the baby do what it has to do." It was a brilliant explanation, not just of midwifery, but of how evangelism works. The Christian's role is that of a servant: "cooperating" with the Spirit on the one hand, "helping" the almost-disciple on the other, not doing too much, not doing too little, helping a natural (or supernatural) process come to its joyful outcome.

EVANGELISM AS TEAMWORK

"This is all very well," you may be saying. "You're an academic, and we all know academics live in a tidy theoretical world. How does your nice, neat definition help those of us who have to live in the real world?" Let me tell you a story. It's a real story, but it could be repeated, with variations, innumerable times.

A few years back, I received an email from someone called Becky. She had been exploring my website and reading some of the evangelistic articles there and had some questions for me. But she said, "I'm just so far away from where I think I ought to be if I become a Christian. I can't imagine that I'll ever be able to (or be willing to) make the changes necessary." She told me she had been living with a married man for fifteen years, and she worked in the gambling industry, where she didn't know of any Christians.

What had prompted this exchange was that a year earlier, Becky's sister had gotten married, and Becky had played the organ for the service. (I should add that she had not learned to play the organ for religious reasons.) The (Anglican) priest, Joanne, asked her if she might be willing to do it regularly, Becky said yes, and they became friends. They would go walking together in the hills around where they lived.

Becky began to ask serious questions about Christianity, did some searching on the web, came across me, and asked me her many questions. In the course of our correspondence, I quoted C. S. Lewis, as I often do. She had never heard of him, despite having been a student at Oxford. I recommended the Narnia stories, and they blew her away. Here are some of her comments:

I found the whole creation scene [in *The Magician's Nephew*] very moving. It has made me realize that rather than simply (!) being created, I've been called to life for a purpose. What have I been created (designed) for? Who am I meant to be?

I've been questioning my work anyway regarding its moral validity; reading about how the dwarves loved making the crowns [in *The Magician's Nephew*] has made me question it in another way: "Where does my passion lie?" "What is it that I have been made to do well?"

How do logic and faith contribute to what I think is the truth? The "seeing is believing" / "believing is seeing" section [in *The Magician's Nephew*; we had talked about this] has raised questions about my reliance on my own reason to understand/believe some things.

The way Aslan accepts people and their failings [in *The Lion, the Witch and the Wardrobe*] has made me understand much better how God accepts us (and question how I accept myself and others).

What are the things that stop me following Aslan even though I believe in him (like Susan in *Prince Caspian*)? This is one I *really* need to work on.

Then Becky moved to another church in the city center. One of the staff at the church, Fran, noticed that she was new and invited her for coffee. They began to meet every two weeks, and the conversation quickly gravitated toward the gospel. Fran, said Becky, was "really helpful but not at all pushy." Eventually, after a conversation with Joanne, Becky became a follower of Jesus. She left the married man and left the gambling industry.

Some time later, she met a Christian widower at church—George—and they got married. My wife and I happened to be in the UK at the time, so we were able to be at the wedding. During the reception, I suggested to Becky that we needed a photo of her "team"—Joanne, Fran, and myself. (C. S. Lewis was otherwise occupied, or he would have been in it too.)

Here's my question: Who evangelized Becky? Fran actually helped her make the decision to follow Jesus, so you could argue that she was the "real" evangelist. But Becky would never have gotten to that point (humanly speaking) without the interactions with Joanne, C. S. Lewis, and myself. We all played a different part. And it's important to know too that this didn't happen quickly. My emails with Becky span seven months, and she had been playing the organ in Joanne's church for a year before that. I would say this is how people normally become disciples: it is a long, slow, winding process, and it involves a wide variety of relationships and experiences. Or as Anne Lamott describes it, "My coming to faith did not start with a leap but rather a series of staggers from what seemed like one safe place to another."[13]

God, who oversees the whole process of evangelism, used all of us in different ways to help Becky move to become a follower of Jesus. The work of evangelism is the work of a team of people in the body of Christ. And when people finally become Christians, then, as Jesus knew, "sower and reaper . . . rejoice together" (John 4:36).[14]

Evangelism therefore means teamwork. Actually, if I were going to revise my definition yet again, I would want to add something to that effect: that evangelism is normally a community effort, a ministry of the whole body of Christ. All sorts of Christians say and do all sorts of things that in the end contribute to the process of someone becoming an apprentice of Jesus. But I think the definition is long enough already. You may not consider yourself an "evangelist"—frankly, most Christians don't—but there is something unique you can contribute to the work of evangelism, as Joanne, Fran, and I did. Oh, and C. S. Lewis too.

GIFTS OF EVANGELISM

We can think of it this way. Some people's contribution to the process of evangelism is simply showing the love of Christ—I did promise we would get to this—taking around a casserole when someone is sick, babysitting a child during an emergency, going for a walk with someone, or offering to pray for a neighbor. For others, it is praying for friends and neighbors to come to faith in Jesus. (I sometimes wonder whether anyone becomes a disciple without having been prayed for.) In many cases—think about Becky and Joanne—it is simply being a friend to someone who does not claim to be a Christian. These are all important expressions of the gospel—small tastes of the good news about what God is like. If it helps, we can think of this as "witness," often silent witness, rather than evangelism.

At some point in the process of moving toward Jesus, many people become involved with Christians. It may be a course that teaches basic Christianity, such as Alpha.[15] Or it might be working with a group of Christians who are, in one way or another, doing gospel work in their community—volunteering at a food bank, renting a plot at a church's community garden, or hosting a small group.[16] Whatever it is, it will usually begin with a verbal invitation, or at least a conversation about what is going on.

Sometimes there is an opportunity for us to say something about why we are followers of Jesus. Quite recently, I was with a group of friends who have no church connection, and conversation turned to what motivates us in life. There was some joking and teasing about the relative power of fear and guilt, greed and lust. Then one friend turned to me, away from the main conversation, and said, "So what would you say has motivated you in your life?" I knew this was no longer a joke. I took a deep breath and said, "Well, you may think this is hokey, but I would have to say Jesus." She thought for a moment, then said, "I'd like to ask you more about that some time." And then the conversation moved on. That's the kind of thing I am thinking of.

Then there are some, and I am one of these, who find themselves called upon to try to explain Christian faith to those who have questions. (That's how I got involved with Becky, after all.) And finally, there are those who seem able to invite people to become followers of Jesus. They do so quietly, without drama or undue emotion and certainly without manipulation. I asked one pastor friend who has this gift how often this had happened, and with some embarrassment, he said, "Um, twenty or thirty times, I guess." That really is a gift.

I like to visualize this "evangelistic teamwork" in the form of an inverted triangle. (See figure 6.2.) Why a triangle rather than a simple list? Because in my experience, more people are able to contribute the things nearer to the top of the triangle. Those who help people to commitment, unfortunately, are few in number. I have only played that part a few times in my life. I wish it were more. In general, too, the things nearer the top of the triangle are more likely to involve actions, and those nearer to the bottom are more likely to require talking.

Where do you fit in this triangle of gifts? My guess is that you recognize yourself somewhere. Perhaps you see your role as "showing the love of Christ" (or something else in the triangle), and that's wonderful. But here's another equally important question: Where could you be stronger? Don't be satisfied with showing the love of Christ. Jesus our Trainer is always wanting to challenge

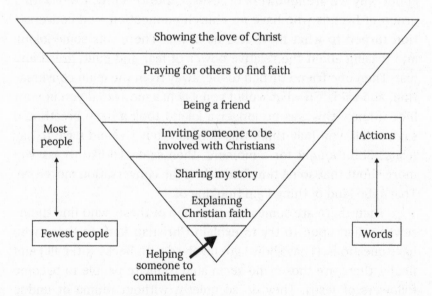

FIGURE 6.2. The teamwork of evangelism

and stretch and grow us. So maybe he wants to encourage you to be someone who prays, or to be a friend (one of the most challenging), or to share your story. Apprenticeship is never doing only the things we find easy.

I want to stress this business of growing in how we contribute to the process of evangelism. The reason is simple. If we translate this image of the triangle into Jesus's metaphor of farming, the things near the top of the triangle would be like clearing stones out of an unplowed field, whereas those near the bottom of the triangle would be the equivalent of reaping. Sometimes I have explained this analogy to church groups and then asked them whether they are best at clearing stones, plowing, sowing seed, watering, or reaping. More than once, to my dismay, the overwhelming majority have said they are called to clear stones out of the field.

You see the problem? I had to move stones out of a field once at a summer camp where we worked, making a space for what would eventually be a sports field. It was backbreaking work in the hot sun, and at the end of a couple of days' work, we had a lovely, stone-free field. But if that was all that happened, a sports field would never have come into being. It would have remained a stone-free field, and before long it would have been taken over by weeds and (eventually) more stones. Clearing stones, in evangelism as in agriculture, is not enough. Someone has to plow, someone has to sow, and only then will someone else be able to reap the harvest.

I didn't make this up. The imagery of sowing and reaping is there in Jesus's parables, of course. But Paul picks it up and takes it a stage further when writing to the church at Corinth. There is squabbling about who is the best Christian leader, and Paul tries to defuse the situation by saying, in effect, that we're all necessary but we all have different roles. Here's how he argues it: "What then is Apollos? What is Paul? Servants through whom you came to believe, as the Lord assigned to each. I planted, Apollos watered, but God gave the growth. So neither the one who plants nor the one who waters is anything, but only God who gives the growth. The one who plants and the one who waters have a common purpose, and each will receive wages according to the labor of each. For we are God's servants, working together; you are God's field, God's building" (1 Cor 3:5–9).

Maybe you are a sower who might grow into a waterer or a waterer who might grow into a reaper. Perhaps you are a reaper who needs to pay more attention to sowing or be more patient of those who "only" move the stones.[17] Paul says God "assigned" our roles. But if we listen carefully, maybe our teacher wants to reassign us. Apprenticeships get more challenging as we go on.

Having said that, I still feel a little uncomfortable spending a whole chapter discussing evangelism. Why? Because all too often it becomes a "thing" that we do—or, more often, don't do. I mentioned earlier one of my favorite definitions of evangelism—that it is "overflow." That makes sense, doesn't it? Rebecca Pippert describes once asking a student whether she felt comfortable about evangelism. "Oh yes," the student replied. "I do it twice a week."[18] It sounds like a faucet: twice a week you turn it on for a time, but then for the rest of the week it's off. This isn't what you would call a natural overflow of the life of Christ.

So the question is not really about evangelism; the question is rather how committed we are to following Jesus. Our daily prayer doesn't need to be "Lord, help me talk to someone today." That doesn't satisfy God: God wants more of us than that—in fact, God wants all of us. As C. S. Lewis explains, "It is not so much of our time and so much of our attention that God demands; it is not even all our time and all our attention; it is ourselves. . . . For He claims all, because He is love and must bless. He cannot bless us unless He has us."[19]

A better prayer would be "Lord, help me be available, help me be totally open, to your Spirit this day, whatever that means, whether evangelism or anything else." Frankly, that's much harder and much scarier. But that's when the life of Christ will overflow from our lives.

EVANGELISM AS SOMETHING TO BE LEARNED

Let me end this chapter with an encouragement. There is one phrase in the scene in Mark 1 that we have not touched on. When Jesus calls the first disciples, he adds, "and I will make you fish for people" (Mark 1:17). "I will make you" could mean one of two things: either "I will force you," as in "I will make you eat your broccoli," or "I will shape you," as in "I will make you into a musician." In saying "I will make you," Jesus means the latter. The Greek word can be translated as "make, manufacture, construct, produce, form, or fashion." So Jesus is saying, "I will shape you into those who know how to fish for people."

I feel I have been stretched and grown in my practice of evangelism over the years. As a young Christian, I was involved in a program that had us preaching in the streets, giving out evangelistic tracts, and going from door to door talking about Jesus and selling Bibles. (I do realize you may put down the book at this point and never pick it up again. But hang in there. That is only the beginning.) I can't quite imagine doing those things now, but I don't regret for one moment doing them. They were done in good faith, nobody got hurt, and maybe some good was done. (I have several times met people who say, somewhat shamefacedly, that they were helped to move toward faith by the words of a street preacher.)

Later on, while on staff with InterVarsity, I learned to lead discussions about Christian faith in cafeterias and studies of the biographies of Jesus (a.k.a. the gospels) in dorm rooms. I organized events where Christian faculty would come and lecture on such topics as "Can an Engineer Be a Christian?" (apparently the answer is yes), or "Is Faith Just a Psychological Crutch?" by a psychology professor (apparently the answer is no), or "Is God Green?" by an ecology professor. (This last reference attracted graffiti where the writer wrote underneath: "No, she's Black.")

The third stage that I can discern was in the 1990s, when I was encouraged to develop a ministry as an itinerant evangelist. I would visit a university campus for a week, at the invitation of the Christian students, and give a series of public lectures about Christianity through the week. Sometimes I would debate with philosophy professors on subjects such as the existence of God or the rationality of faith. Other times I would do lectures illustrated by movie clips[20] or with (what at the time were considered) catchy titles, such as "Jesus Is Alive, Elvis Is Alive: What's the Difference?"[21] It was scary, especially at first, but gradually I grew into it.

Now I think the challenge is quite different: to know how to be a good evangelist in less structured situations, in natural friendships, and in everyday conversation. It may seem to you that that is where I should have begun years ago, but Jesus's curriculum is tailored to each of us individually, and this one seems to have been right for me.

I hope you will have picked up this message already: don't worry that your experience in evangelism is different from mine. Of course it is. It's meant to be different. But for each of us, apprenticeship in the ways of the kingdom will stretch us and grow us in ways we probably cannot anticipate. And some of those will certainly involve evangelism, as Jesus makes us "fish for people." Yes, he wants us to learn forgiveness, generosity, inclusiveness, patience, and so on. But of equal importance is helping others become disciples, which does not come about without evangelism. In other words, evangelism is one of the things you learn in the school of Jesus.

EVANGELISM AND THE EVANGEL

Well, I rest my case. I am convinced the heart of evangelism is the verbal communication of the gospel and everything that goes along with that. But the connection with the theme of a church shaped by the gospel goes deeper than that.

The Greek word for gospel is *euangelion*, from which we get the word *evangel*, so in theory evangel is at the heart of evangelism. But sadly, it is quite possible for those things "which God has joined together" to "be put asunder."[22] Indeed, what is so off-putting to people is the fact that evangelism doesn't always incorporate—incarnate—the nature of the gospel. The good news needs to be communicated in a way that in itself conveys what the gospel is, a way that actually gives a foretaste of the gospel even before it is believed.

Think back to Becky's story. Joanne and Fran both extended friendship to her, and in that friendship, she began to experience the welcoming love of God. When she and I were emailing, I tried to be patient with her questions and to explain what I understood of the gospel in a gentle and noncoercive way. This, too, I hoped (and prayed) would show her something of the reality of Christ. And the Narnia stories touched her, not just with propositions about the gospel, but with the reality of Aslan's love and calling.

So although I have emphasized that evangelism means words—and I believe it does—those words need to be spoken in a way that in itself carries the alluring aroma of Christ.[23] Words and actions need to speak in harmony.

CHAPTER 7

THE GOSPEL AND CULTURE
Created, Damaged, Restored

Contemporary Western culture has perhaps the strongest sense of personal identity in the history of the world. We say things like "Be who you are!" "Be your own person!" "Don't worry what other people think: do what you want to do!" and "You do you!" We tend to think these are absolutes, applicable to anyone, anywhere, at any time. But are they?

The apostle Paul certainly didn't think that way. See what you notice about his sense of self in these words:

> Though I am free with respect to all, I have made myself a slave to all, so that I might win more of them. To the Jews I became as a Jew, in order to win Jews. To those under the law I became as one under the law (though I myself am not under the law) so that I might win those under the law. To those outside the law I became as one outside the law (though I am not free from God's law but am under Christ's law) so that I might win those outside the law. To the weak I became weak, so that I might win the weak. I have become all things to all people, that I might by all means save some. I do it all for the sake of the gospel, so that I may share in its blessings. (1 Cor 9:19–23)

To be honest, to me his attitude here makes him sound like a spiritual chameleon. One day he is a Jew, another a gentile; one day a servant,[1] another day "weak." What? Who exactly is this? Does he have no solid identity of his own that he has to adapt so radically to different groups? Whatever happened to "be your own person"?

Before we jump into this, I can't help noticing the last sentence of Paul's thought. Whatever it is that he is saying here about his selfhood, he is clear about the reason: what he is doing is "for the sake of the gospel." It's a phrase that occurs in only one other place in the New Testament, and it is on the lips of Jesus: "Those who want to save their life will lose it, and those who lose their life for my sake, and *for the sake of the gospel*, will save it" (Mark 8:35; italics mine). To do something for the sake of the gospel is actually to do something for Jesus. And the "something" Jesus specifies is losing our life. Well, that sheds a light on Paul's odd statement. If "my self" is not at the heart of "my life," what is? So for Paul to do what might appear to us to be compromising his personal integrity, not to "be himself," the motivation has to be pretty strong—and it is. His motive is the strongest. He does it for the gospel. Let's dig into what that might mean.

What about the popular advice we give: "Be your own person"? Paul was certainly not "his own person." If you could explain to him what you meant by the phrase (and that would be a challenge in itself), such a thought would horrify him. Human beings are not created to "be their own person." To belong to yourself is a pretty good shorthand definition of hell. No, people are made to belong to God and to be servants of Jesus Christ. That's where we get our true identity; that's the integration point for our personality.

It is precisely because Paul knows who he is "in Christ" that he can say what he says about adapting to different cultures. Of course, we all modify our behavior and speech according to the culture we find ourselves in, often unconsciously. When I moved from Britain to Canada over forty years ago, I quickly learned that a request for a glass of "wohtah" would elicit puzzled looks and that if I really wanted water, I should ask for a glass of "waahderr." Life is full of such adaptations. And they do not threaten our identity.

Of course, what Paul means is rather more radical. You can see something of what he meant from his sermons in Acts. On the one hand, when he preaches to a Jewish audience, his Jewish self comes to the forefront. This audience respects the authority of Scripture; they see eye to eye with him on topics like the nature of God, of sin, of atonement, and other major issues, and so Paul's sermons to the Jews build on that common ground. When he addresses a gentile audience, however, as he does at Athens (Acts 17:16–34), he does something totally different.[2] He does a good imitation of a cultured Greek, and he draws on what he knows of his audience's culture—their worship, their philosophy, their poetry. He doesn't quote pagan philosophers to his Jewish audience, and neither does he reason about the fulfilment of Scripture with Greek thinkers. The Jews would be offended; the Greeks would scoff.[3]

In other words, Paul doesn't hesitate to adapt to the culture he is in, but not because he is unsure of himself. Precisely the opposite. As you read Paul's letters, the sense of a strong personality clearly comes through. Rowan Williams describes Paul as "[a] passionate man, powerfully, even overwhelmingly, impressive in some ways."[4] Paul knows the story he inhabits and knows something of the role he plays in that story. The gospel has made him who he is, so he is not fearful of different cultures, or of embracing their realities, in order to share that same gospel with others.

How then do we think about "culture"? In particular, how does a grasp of the gospel help us live and communicate in different cultures? What we need is a theological understanding of culture. That might sound intimidating, but it isn't really. A theology of anything is simply how we understand that thing in the light of Christian belief, whether work, sex, the environment—or culture. So let's consider culture through the lenses of four cardinal Christian ideas: creation and sin (which I will discuss together), then incarnation, and finally the end of the world—eschatology. Work with me.

BEGINNING AT THE BEGINNING

Long ago, when I was a theological student, I remember my Old Testament professor, Alec Motyer, saying, "Every Christian doctrine is an aspect of the doctrine of creation."[5] I am still processing that. He meant, for example, that we won't understand sin unless we understand that God created the world and made us stewards of it. We won't understand redemption unless we understand the idea of renewing all that is broken in the created world. You get the idea. By the same token, when we start to think about culture and a Christian approach to it, that also begins with creation.

Here then is a place to begin: All of creation is intended to reflect the glory, love, beauty, and harmony of God. This includes human beings. Yet we are created not just as individuals but as social beings to live in community, the kind of community that reflects the beauty and harmony of the Trinity.

The challenge is that whenever two or more human beings are together and start interacting, they have to figure out some ways of relating in order to survive and thrive. That interaction forms the most basic building block of culture. Archbishop Derek Worlock once defined culture as "the way we do things round here."[6] There are longer, more sophisticated definitions of culture, of course, but for my money that one is difficult to beat. As soon as two people decide (say) to eat together, there will have to be some agreements as to how they do it. Fingers or forks? Chairs or floor? Meat or vegetables? How many courses? Is it polite or rude to belch? Once they reach these agreements, they have the makings of a culture. But if the two are then joined by a third, first of all the new person will have to learn how the original two "do things round here"—but in all likelihood, that "way" will change somewhat if the third is to be accommodated.[7] And so culture evolves.

All this is a long way around to say a very simple thing: God has made us enculturated beings. There is no acultural community and no acultural reality. Sometimes Christians recoil in horror at the idea that they might be "influenced by culture." I once heard a theological student exclaim, "I hope they don't start bringing *culture* into the chapel!"—as though there was no "culture" there already. Seminary chapels, like every other institution, have very distinctive, even idiosyncratic, cultures. If we forget that we inhabit a culture—or, to be more accurate, many cultures simultaneously—the danger is that we begin to treat our own culture (or cultures) as an absolute and as normative for all human beings.

Frankly, there is no other option for human beings than to be immersed in culture, just as fish have no choice but to be immersed in water—if they want to live. To be a cultural being is not an unfortunate necessity but part of the glory of being human. Cultures are simply the ways human beings have figured out to organize their lives. In a world without sin and evil, those cultures would always reflect the glory of God and enable human flourishing in the image of God. To be cultural is as much a part of being authentically human as is having a body.

Yet this is not a world without sin and evil, and not everything in the cultural garden is rosy. Sin's grubby fingers extend everywhere. Because of sin, all cultures fail in their calling. They mar the glory of God and prevent human flourishing. As a result, as Newbigin puts it, "we have to say both 'God accepts human culture' and also 'God judges human culture.'"[8] What Indigenous archbishop Mark MacDonald says of his culture is true of all: "Indigenous societies are, like all other societies, under the rule and authority of God. They are, like all other human societies, places of good and bad, nurture and trouble, promise and problem."[9] We should not reject culture, even if we could, but we are right to feel ambivalent about it. Fish don't "reject" water, though they may sense when the water is contaminated—and when they don't, the water can kill them.[10]

This is not the end of the story, however—thank God. God has not written off human culture, any more than God has written off human beings or the created world. Remember the gospel? God's determination to redeem, restore, and renew all things through Christ? If everything is redeemable, and if human beings are designed to live together, then culture is one of those things that will need to be redeemed, since how we live together is . . . culture.

The ultimate proof of God's affirmation of culture lies, like everything else, in Jesus Christ and his good news. How come?

GOD'S SELF-INCULTURATION

When God enters human history to redeem humankind, God enters a specific culture in history, with all its beauty and all its fallenness. God in Jesus lives a certain way, dresses and eats a certain way, speaks particular languages (certainly Aramaic, but possibly Hebrew and Greek as well), and worships as his culture worships. Come to think of it, if God is going to enter history and become human, even God has no option other than to become a creature of a specific culture. This is the way God has made the world. Even for God, "incarnate and acultural" would be an oxymoron. The incarnation honors the reality of culture and being part of a culture. Incarnation says, "It is OK, indeed it is good, to live in a culture." We can go so far as to say that "The incarnation is God's self-inculturation in this world."[11]

This is what is sometimes called "the scandal of particularity"[12]: somehow it would seem easier if God had spoken in timeless universal truths from heaven, without getting God's hands dirty. It is the hands of God, dirtied by the earth of first-century Palestine, that are the "scandal." But then, we have no way of hearing or understanding "universal truths," since we have no universal language, and in any case, we would inevitably filter those universal truths through our own culturally conditioned minds and understand them differently. Yet once those truths are translated into a human language, they have become culture specific, and people who don't know that language won't understand them. Culture enables communication—but limits it at the same time.

We also need to bear in mind Newbigin's caution that God both affirms and judges culture. Thus while Jesus embraces fully the glory and the particularities of first-century Mideastern culture, he also makes clear his displeasure at the way things are being "done round here," not least by the religious leaders, who are not exactly promoting human flourishing.

But that does not undermine the basic commitment to culture per se; it merely underlines the fact that it is worth restoring. Indeed, as Jesus gathers apprentices around him and teaches them a new way of relating to God and to himself, to one another and to the world, he is himself creating a new culture, a new way of doing things round here, that is intended as a model for all cultures.

THE END OF CULTURE

Having said that culture is a mixture of the good, the bad, and the ugly, I want to take this question of the restoration of culture a step further. Here's a crucial clue. At the very end of the Bible, Revelation speaks of a "new Jerusalem, coming down out of heaven from God" (Rev 21:2). This suggests that the final destiny of human beings is something created by God and given by God, quite independent of us. That makes sense.

But then, a little further on is a strange statement, made twice, that suggests the city is not all God's work after all: "The kings of the earth will bring their glory into it" (Rev 21:24) and "people will bring into it the glory and the honor of the nations" (Rev 21:26). At first sight, this sounds very strange: the thought that anything from our present world (which has "passed away" according to Rev 21:1) could be brought into God's new city. It sounds almost like desecration. Wouldn't our "glory" mess up God's perfect creation all over again? Wouldn't it detract from God's glory? Apparently not.

The question, of course, is what *glory* means. On one level, it simply means the "essential character" of something. God's glory is what God is essentially like. When we "glorify" God, we are not adding anything to God. We are just acknowledging God's love, God's holiness, God's justice, God's patience, God's salvation—thinking about it, singing about it, and being very thankful for it!

But we human beings have our glory too. In different parts of the Bible, various things are said to be human glory. Proverbs provides several examples. Our "glory" may be our strength (Prov 20:29), or our willingness to forgive (Prov 19:11), or our desire to investigate things (Prov 25:2). These are things to marvel at and to praise because they are glorious.

It will not come as a surprise, however, to realize that those things that are glorious in us are merely reflections of the glories of God: we are made in God's image, after all, "crowned . . . with glory and honor" (Ps 8:5). Thus we are most glorious when we most resemble God, when the image of Jesus is most fully formed in us: our glory is his glory. It does not originate with us; it is never more than reflected glory (2 Cor 3:18). And here, of course, is the gospel again. The work the gospel does in us is precisely this: to restore us to the likeness and glory of God.

But we tend to assume that the glory of God's image is seen only in individuals. But what if it can also be seen in communities—and cultures—where God is honored and served?

That brings us back to the "glory of the nations." Presumably it means the "essential character" of each nation. Andy Crouch suggests that "the glory of a nation is simply its greatest and most distinctive cultural achievement."[13] Just as individuals reflect different nuances of the God who created them, so presumably can different churches, different communities . . . or different nations. Maybe there is something Nicaraguan about God, something Malaysian, something Kenyan, something Welsh.

A friend who was an Anglican priest in the Arctic for many years commented, "The 'glory' of the culture of the Inuit was the respect for their environment and the natural life which sustained them, along with the fundamental principle of sharing to sustain the whole community."[14]

And that distinctive "glory," when shaped by the gospel, is reflected in each nation's music, its art, its education, its science and technology, its law, its customs, its dance—what Richard Middleton calls "the best of human workmanship that has been developed through history."[15]

If this is right, then what John is saying here is that this "glory" will be welcomed into God's new city, duly cleansed of anything unworthy, and given a place of honor in the new creation. The responsibility that God gave to humankind at the beginning to be stewards of creation—what is sometimes called "the cultural mandate"—is now seen to have eternal significance. Wherever God's glory is seen in human culture, it will last forever.

As Earl Palmer puts it,

The uniqueness of each person and tribe is preserved as part of their glory just as the unique colors of the jewels are preserved as part of their glory. . . . Yes, by all means, work hard on your research into the wonders of plasma physics, and plan on continuing that study into the new order. That research is part of the glory and honor of your ethnos.[16] So are your relationship with children, parents, friends; so are your hobbies and avocations—as is also the color of your skin and eyes. . . . God who made us and redeemed us will raise us up again. He will fulfill us and all the created order too.[17]

You can probably see already how this is connected to our theme of the gospel. After all, if the gospel is the announcement of the kingdom, that God is restoring all the broken things of God's world—"people and things, animals and atoms"—isn't John's vision simply the glorious climax of all that work that God has been doing? Revelation's picture of the new creation would be less than perfect without this living proof of the success of God's plan—but perfect is what it is, and that perfection includes "the glory of the nations."

Don't you find this encouraging? It means that when we spend time on what Crouch calls "culture-making," trying to apply the ways of the gospel to "the way we do things round here," we are not wasting our time on something that will end up on the universe's garbage heap. What we do now, in as far as it shows the glory of God, is honored in the new world.

BEING DISCERNING ABOUT CULTURE

The gospel then gives us a framework for a theology of culture. The doctrines of creation, incarnation, redemption, and eschatology all show culture to be a good thing, damaged by our independence from God and able to be reshaped and restored by the good news of the gospel.

What does this mean for living out the gospel and talking about the gospel in any given culture? Let's start at the beginning:

It is not just an unfortunate pragmatic necessity that Christians have to figure out how the gospel relates to any given culture. It is a thing to be celebrated. God's intention is that every culture should reflect the glory of God—not because God is a power-hungry dictator but because for culture to be shaped in God's way fulfils the purpose for which we were made and enables us to flourish.

The gospel therefore has to be carefully translated—adapted, if you like, even incarnated—into those cultures in order to make clear how it blesses them (because they are good) and challenges them (because they fall short of the norms of the kingdom). If we make it inaccessible by insisting on our own cultural expression of it, we make it unintelligible to them, and it is no longer good news from God.

NONNEGOTIABLE BARRIERS

Having said that, there will always be obstacles to the gospel, and some are intrinsic to the nature of the gospel itself. In that sense, there is nothing we can do to modify them, whatever the culture. We have to be faithful as well as flexible.

The gospel comes with its own inherent challenges. They are not imposed arbitrarily by God just to make our lives difficult. They are created by our own resistance and the against-the-grain nature of the gospel. Remember, for example, that the gospel calls us to repent and believe. To repent is to give up our natural independence, and to believe is to commit to following Jesus's leadership instead of doing our own thing. There is no getting away from the fact that this is tough and (I don't think I speak only for myself in saying) is an orientation of life that needs renewing every day. Then there is the reality that at the heart of God's redemption is the death of Jesus. That is a challenge too. As Paul experienced, the centrality of the crucifixion for Christian faith is universally a "stumbling block," both to religious folk and to intellectuals (1 Cor 1:23).[18] So I am not proposing the abolition of all barriers to the gospel. There are some that are unavoidable because they are an essential part of the message itself.

BARRIERS OF OUR OWN MAKING

On the other hand, it is quite possible for us to impose requirements of our own devising. I remember, for instance, one (suppos-
edly) evangelistic sermon that ended with the suggestion that if
you want to follow Jesus, the first requirement is to believe in the
infallibility, inerrancy, and supreme authority of the Bible. Um, I'm
not sure where the preacher found that as part of the New Testament's gospel.

For messengers of the gospel to create extra barriers,
unthinkingly or even willfully, out of human preference and inflexible tradition is intolerable. Why is this so bad? The danger is that,
when the gospel is too closely identified with a particular culture,
the hearers in another culture may not hear it as good news—for
all the wrong reasons. It may be tempting to say they have rejected
it out of their hardness of heart, but the stronger possibility is
that they have never "heard" the gospel in any meaningful sense—
because of its cultural trappings. What they are rejecting, if anything, is the culture of the evangelists, not the gospel itself.

Missionaries over the centuries have always realized this. One
of my favorite stories concerns Jesuit Robert de Nobili, missionary
to India in the sixteenth century. He discovered that the Brahmins
understood the gospel as an invitation to become Portuguese. To
them, the ideas of "Christian" and "Portuguese" were so closely
identified that they were indistinguishable. They assumed that
embracing Christianity would also mean abandoning their Brahmin
culture and learning to dress, speak, and eat as the Portuguese did.

So what did de Nobili do? Instead of requiring them to adapt
to his culture, he adapted to their culture, and in quite radical ways.
He entered fully into Brahmin culture—living with them, learning
their language, adopting their dress, memorizing their poetry (in
some cases better than they did), and cutting himself off from his
fellow countrymen. It was said that the only remnant of Western
culture he retained was an insistence on importing Communion
wine from Europe. What happened? Over the course of the following four years, he baptized over one thousand Brahmins.[19] Why?
Because once they could tune in to the message of the gospel and

hear its invitation and its challenge clearly, without radio interference from an alien culture, it was deeply attractive and had nothing to do with "becoming Portuguese."

In a very deep sense, de Nobili did a very Jesus-like thing. We could paraphrase Paul's description of Jesus's incarnation and say that de Nobili "did not count being [Portuguese] as a thing to be grasped, but emptied himself, taking the form of a [Brahmin]" (see Phil 2:5–8). Jesus's incarnation is always a model for effective missionaries. Indeed, it is the only model.

This is hardly a new idea. As we have seen, Paul lived this way, as did missionaries like de Nobili who followed his model. Over the centuries, the church has spelled out these same principles from time to time.[20] How the history of world missions might have been different if those guidelines had been observed!

SHOULDN'T THE CHURCH BE SEPARATE FROM CULTURE?

Before we leave this topic, there are important questions that always arise in the gospel-and-culture discussion and that deserve a response.

In recent years I have noticed a move away from the kind of sympathy for culture that I am recommending here.[21] In part, this is a healthy reaction against Christendom, the long period when the church by and large identified too closely with "the culture." Trying to be "relevant" at all costs is necessarily a bad thing.

The thinking is that if Christendom led to the betrayal of gospel principles, then for the church to recover its authentic character, we need to distance ourselves from the dominant culture. Walter Brueggemann was one of the first to name this as a problem: "The contemporary American church is so largely enculturated to the American ethos of consumerism, that it has little power to believe or act. . . . The internal cause of such enculturation is our loss of identity through the abandonment of the faith tradition. . . . It is the task of prophetic ministry to bring the claims of the tradition and the situation of enculturation into an effective interface."[22]

That makes good sense. As a result, a key question has become, "If the church is not chaplain to the culture, what exactly is it?" And the answer has been that the church is a distinct society, with its own norms, its own culture ("the way we do things round here"), and its own way of thinking and talking—its own "grammar"—with all of this shaped by the gospel.[23]

This movement to rediscover the church's true nature can be traced back to the great twentieth century German theologian Karl Barth,[24] and not least to his part in the leadership of what was called the "Confessing Church"—the alliance of churches that refused to collaborate with the Nazis in Germany during the Second World War.[25] There is the church's opposition to culture in its strongest form—for entirely understandable and laudable reasons.[26]

I find this a compelling argument. In fact, the whole thesis of this book—the view that everything to do with the church is shaped by the gospel—has been deeply shaped by this kind of outlook. At the same time, it has its own dangers. One is a question of what God is like (a theological danger) and the other a question of what human nature is like (a pragmatic danger).

THE THEOLOGICAL PROBLEM

I was talking to a church planter friend of mine in Kenya, John Njuguna, and asked him how many churches he had planted. He began counting on his fingers but ran out. I asked him how he did it. He told me he would move into a new community where he hoped to start a new church. Then he would talk with the local people and ask them what they thought God is like. I have always thought that's a brilliant question to begin with, better than "Are you saved?" or even "Do you know who Jesus is?" It is perhaps the most important question we can ever ask.[27] It is certainly a good way to begin a church. My answer, as I have tried to argue, is that "we know what God is like from the gospel."

My fear about the "keep-church-separate-from-culture" impulse is that it gives a partially correct answer to the question. It says, "God is shaping a new community called the church, which will live in a distinctive way and be a witness to the gospel in the world." So far so good.

But it neglects another aspect of God, which is equally important: God is also at work outside the church. God is already communicating with people and drawing them—through nature, through culture, through conscience, through experiences of love and beauty and art, through human nature itself—long before church gets there. This reality has traditionally been called "common grace." John Wesley found a different phrase for it, calling it God's "prevenient grace." I like that because the "pre-" draws attention to the fact that grace is at work in people *before* they hear the gospel. God is always and everywhere "before." That grace is the work of God's Spirit, preparing people's hearts and minds to "repent and believe."[28]

Traditionally, theologians have distinguished between "common grace"—God's care for all of creation whether or not people believe in God[29]—and "special grace," the deeper understanding of God that comes primarily through the gospel.[30] It seems to me that the keep-church-separate-from-culture instinct stresses special grace and neglects the reality of common grace. And that changes everything. It affects not only how we understand how God works through the gospel (inside the church only or inside *and* outside?) but also what it means to be the church in the world (where do we put our energies—inside only or inside *and* outside?).

Certainly, there may be times when Christians have to make a radical separation between themselves and the culture around them, to be what Richard Mouw calls "cultural eunuchs."[31] No question about it. German Christians during the Second World War felt that in respect to Nazism.[32] But for some, strangely enough, the experience of Nazism had the opposite effect. Mouw points out that in Holland at least, "the shared experience of standing against a common foe with people of different religious and non-religious beliefs . . . stirred up feelings of social solidarity that did not simply disappear when the war ended."[33]

That in turn led to a fresh appreciation of the wideness of God's common grace. So in some ways, that war led different groups of Christians to emphasize different sides of the antithesis.

In general, though there can be exceptions, I have no hesitation in saying that God is at work in so-called secular culture and that whatever God does and wherever God does it, it is good. And common grace prepares the ground for the gospel.[34]

Even Karl Barth seems to have softened his hard-line stance by the end of his life, once the threat of Nazism was over. He speaks of "secular parables," places in secular culture where the truth of God (as measured by Christ and by Scripture, of course) is to be found, pointing people toward the gospel.[35]

THE PRAGMATIC PROBLEM

My other concern is that the emphasis on the unique identity of the church, crucial though it is, easily leads to introspection and thinking mainly about the internal life of the church, not least the finer points of liturgical correctness. The argument may take the following form: "If we get our internal life in order, that is all the witness that is needed." Or the view may be somewhat more outward looking: "Once we get our internal life in order, only then will we be equipped to go out as a witness to the world." Both views are seductive but ultimately misleading. Why? In the one case, because a witness has to be audible and visible, not shut away in the four walls of the church. The witness has to show up in court! And in the other, because our life together will never be up to scratch. The likelihood that one day we will say, "Ah, now after all these years, we are finally ready to look outward" is almost zero.

Spending too much effort on our internal life also underestimates the power of sin. As Anselm warned us nine hundred years ago, "You have not yet considered how grave sin is."[36] The natural tendency of human beings—and that includes churches—is to turn inward. Luther saw that as the essence of sin, calling it "humans turned in on" themselves.[37] And the well-meaning impulse to get our own house in order before looking outward all too easily turns into ecclesiological narcissism.

How can this tension between getting our own house in order (inward looking) and engaging in God's mission (outward looking) be resolved? I believe there is actually a healthy symbiosis between these two things. Our worship together, however imperfect, should inspire and shape us to work with God in God's mission. Remember, for example, how the sacraments of baptism and communion speak of both our relationship with Jesus *and* our involvement in his mission. Both sacraments are gospel shaped, and that which is gospel shaped will always end up sending us out in engagement. And conversely, our involvement in God's mission will drive us back to worship for strength, forgiveness, and direction.

THE SPIRITUAL DISCIPLINE OF BALLET

Finally, an illustration. How do we manage to be firm (about essentials) and flexible (to cultural realities)? Here is how one theological educator puts it: "A persistent misunderstanding . . . has been that openness and cultural sympathy are the enemies of doctrine and discipline. But of course it is not so: learn a lesson from the backbone, all hard definition, which makes possible the bend of the ballerina or the leap of the athlete. So my vision is simply this: interlocking vertebrae of Scripture, the faith of the creeds, and traditional spiritual disciplines will be [for Christians] the conditions for the possibility of every kind of flex required in the coming years."[38]

So yes, there is a spine of the gospel. But if we are clear about that and keep it strong, we can with confidence bend and flex according to our circumstances. The ballet dancer as an image of the cross-cultural Christian. That's a keeper.

CHAPTER 8

THE GOSPEL AND INHERITED CHURCHES

Moving to Missional

We have talked a lot about "*the* church." The church and mission. The church and discipleship. The church and culture. Now we are going to make what might seem like a huge shift and talk about "churches." That might seem a bit of an anticlimax. Up to now, we have thought about God's glorious renewal of the cosmos through Jesus Christ, and the role of the church in that renewal. Now, however, we are going to talk about Springfield Community Church[1] and the struggles of the thirty-four remaining elderly members, in particular their upcoming vote on what color the new sanctuary carpet should be. Well, maybe not that exactly, but that kind of thing. You get the idea.

This may seem incongruous, but it isn't. The local church is where it is at. The local church is where the theological rubber meets the missional road. If all this theory doesn't work here, then it doesn't work anywhere. There is nowhere else to look. This is the only laboratory where the theory is being applied. We cannot talk about that grandiose, abstract thing called "the universal church" if there is no local church. Lesslie Newbigin saw this very clearly: "How is it possible that the gospel should be credible, that people should come to believe that the power which has the last word in human affairs is represented by a man hanging on a cross? I am suggesting that the only answer, the only hermeneutic of the gospel, is a congregation of men and women who believe it and live by it."[2] In other words, why should people believe the gospel? Not because they read a book of brilliant apologetics (though that may happen) or because they catch a vision of what the church "ought to be" but because they see it being worked out in a specific local church—and yes, even Springfield Community Church.

INHERITED CHURCHES

You may know that the world divides into two groups: those who divide the world into two groups and those who don't. For some purposes, I find it useful to belong to the first group. So for the moment, I want to divide churches into two groups, though I do realize it's not always that clear-cut: new churches and, well, "old churches" sounds a bit dismissive, so let me use a term coined by Rowan Williams—"inherited" churches.[3] (After all, who doesn't like to inherit something?) I will talk about new churches in the next chapter. For the moment, let's talk about inherited churches.

The median size of a congregation in North America is seventy-five people.[4] And the number of older people is gradually increasing, while the proportion of younger people is decreasing: In 2006–7, 30 percent of regular attenders in the average congregation were older than age sixty, compared with 25 percent in 1998. The percentage of regular adult participants younger than age thirty-five in the average congregation dropped from 25 percent to 20 percent.[5]

I doubt this comes as a great surprise to most church members. Is there anything small, aging, shrinking churches can do to change things? Yes—and this chapter will address some of them.

At this point, however, we need to be cautious. It is all too easy to talk and act as though survival is the name of the game— the only thing inherited churches should care about. But survival should never be the central issue for a church. After all, what did Jesus say about survival? Well, to be blunt, he was not very sympathetic. Remember his words: "Those who want to save their life will lose it, and those who lose their life for my sake, and for the sake of the gospel, will save it" (Mark 8:35). You want to survive—that is, to save your life or your church's life? According to Jesus, that is the one thing absolutely guaranteed to cause death—to lose your life. Which is precisely what we were trying to avoid.

TWO KINDS OF DEATH

So is there a way for us to survive? Yes, there is, but it is totally counterintuitive. Jesus says, in effect, "You want to save your life? In that case, give it away!" What might that look like? Often we apply these words on an individual level: What does it mean for me personally to lay down my life? Quite apart from the question of laying down my life in a total, physical sense, through martyrdom (and that still happens, of course), what might his teaching mean for the rest of us?

Well, if I think of my "life" as consisting of my time, my love, my talents, my possessions, and so on, what does it mean for me to lay down those things for the cause of Jesus and the good news? That is a good question, the type of question an apprentice ought to be asking every day. This is the way of the gospel.

But what if we apply this question on a community level? What might it mean for a local congregation to lay down its life for Jesus? Well, here too we can ask, Of what does our church's "life" consist? As with individuals, there are various aspects to this—our building, our bank account, our services, our community—and that's just for a start.

Let's begin with the church building. After all, even though some of us were taught from childhood that "the church is people," think how often we say things like "I have a meeting at the church tonight," and we mean the building.[6] Our communal "life" depends on the building, doesn't it? Oh no, there's a challenging thought already. Surely Jesus would never ask us to "lay down" our ownership of our building for the sake of the gospel? Unfortunately, we can't second-guess what specific things Jesus might ask us to "lay down." Lots of churches do not have a building of their own, and others have had to abandon their building for one reason or another, so it wouldn't be wise to be dogmatic about our "need" for a building.

Second, our bank account is pretty important. We couldn't do without that, could we? Well, could we? Third, we need our pattern of weekly worship services, the kind of worship music we like, the kind of liturgy (or lack of liturgy) we prefer, the length of the sermons, and the kind of sermon we like. Fourth, we value our relationships with one another. In a healthy church, we feel like family to one another. So that's definitely a big part of our "life."[7]

Oh goodness, you see where this is going? It looks as though all those things could potentially be on Jesus's chopping block. "But Jesus," we cry, "those are all the things that make up our life as a church! Without them, who would we be? We would curl up and die." And he says, "Um, were you listening just now?"

This doesn't necessarily mean that the key to survival is to give up our building, our bank account, our liturgy, and our community, tomorrow. But his teaching does suggest what our attitude should be toward these things.

Early in my Christian life, I was taught a principle that I continue to find helpful, that I need to "keep my life on an open palm before Jesus." My life, and the things that make it up, all belong to him anyway—he made them and he redeemed them—so what might he want to do with them? He probably doesn't want to take away everything (they were his gift in the first place, after all; it's not a mistake that I have those things), but I do need to keep my hand open and resist the temptation to close my fingers over those things as though they belong to me. They don't.

The question for inherited churches is, How can we best serve the gospel that brought us into existence in the first place? After all, Jesus's words point out that "losing our lives" is not a good thing in itself—it is only good and life-giving if it is "for [Jesus's] sake, and for the sake of the gospel"[8] (Mark 8:35). Doing things for Jesus is doing things for the gospel, and doing things for the gospel is doing them for Jesus.

What Jesus is referring to is a good kind of death. I will try to spell out what that might mean as the chapter goes on and we discuss some of the things we may need to "lay down" to better represent the gospel. But there is another kind of death. I resist calling it "a bad kind of death." Perhaps "a natural death" would be a better phrase.

We have to face the fact that not every church will survive. Churches do not necessarily last forever. Some, of course, last for hundreds or even thousands of years. An English bishop told me not long ago of being at two celebrations of churches that were each marking nine hundred years of worship and service. But there is no theological reason churches or even denominations must survive. One Canadian denomination is closing fifty churches every year—virtually one every week.[9] Not that this is a new or even a Western phenomenon. Philip Jenkins wrote a book describing how whole vast denominations that once existed in the Middle East (and that most of us have never heard about) no longer exist.[10]

Churches die a natural death for different reasons. Sometimes it is simply demographic: people move away and nobody is left. Sometimes a church ceases to be sensitive to the needs of its community, becomes inward looking, and withers away. Sometimes it is merely a matter of age: church members realize that the needed changes are beyond either their energy or their resources, and the churches close. Of course, this means we need church leaders who are specially gifted and trained to give palliative care to dying congregations. (I will say more about this ministry in chapter 10.) This will never be a popular vocation, but it is an honorable one and much needed.

But let's start by being positive. What can inherited churches do to find new life? I have six suggestions. There is no guarantee that any of these will save Springfield Community Church, of course, but that's not why we do these things: they are the right things for Christians to do anyway, and we trust God for the rest.

1. Don't Beat Yourself Up

The changes in church life over the past fifty years have, in large measure, been caused by shifts in Western culture that began three hundred years ago and over which we have had little or no control. And because churches in general could do little or nothing to prevent these changes, there is absolutely no point in beating ourselves up about them. I think I can say with confidence that nothing the thirty-four members of Springfield Community Church could have done over their lifetimes would have turned back the tide of secularism in the West.

There are many parallels. Think, for instance, of the post office. I was at boarding school for two years before going to university, and every Sunday night, I sat down and wrote my parents several pages describing (in selective detail, I admit) the doings of the previous week. My mother kept the letters, each one still in its envelope, until the day she died—and I have now inherited them. I plan to leave them to my children. It goes without saying that they will leave no such legacy for their children.

The decline of letter writing has had major consequences for the postal services in most Western countries. In big cities, the old post office building is often an imposing classical edifice, representing the status of the mail service in the community. In Britain, it is even called the *Royal* Mail, to stress its importance. Now it is more likely to be a little counter hidden away at the back of a drug store.

So what did the postal service do wrong? The simple reality is that, like churches, the postal services were overtaken by cultural and technological shifts beyond their control. Why write a letter if you can send an email or a text? No paper needed, no pen, no envelope, no stamp, and (most importantly) no delay in its getting there—or (if you are lucky) in getting a reply. As a result, postal services in the Western world are struggling to reinvent themselves— but the jury is still out as to whether they can survive.

That doesn't mean churches have always done everything right—far from it—so let's repent of those things as the Holy Spirit brings them to our awareness. Neither does it mean that we can do nothing to change our own situation, as you will see. But let's not move into the future dragged down by a false sense of guilt and failure.

2. Teach the Gospel

Have I mentioned that I think the gospel is central to the church's life and work? If I am right, then the key to the church's recovery lies not in new strategies for growth (though they have a place) or in "restructuring" (usually a euphemism for closures and mergers) but in a fresh conviction that the good news really is amazingly good.

If the goodness of the gospel begins to seep into our minds and hearts, things will change. Not least because the gospel is about God's love seeking to change everything, we will begin to ask not just what it means for ourselves but what it means for those outside the walls. If the gospel is given free rein, it will reorder relationships, budget priorities, leadership, and programs. The gospel promises to make all things new: that's a paradigm shift like no other.

You may remember Luther's definition of sin, that it is human-kind turned in on itself. Unfortunately, this turning-in affects not only the world in general but churches too. Here is how Judy Paulsen puts it: "Churches rarely develop self-absorption inten-tionally. They fall into a self-centered focus over a period of sev-eral years; it simply becomes a habit. Changing this perspective requires intentionality on the part of church leaders."[11]

The gospel by its very nature addresses that problem and turns us outward. So once we begin to grasp that, what can we do to remedy that tendency? Bishop John Taylor wrote, "Mission is finding out what God is doing and trying to do it with him."[12] If that is correct, the first step is to find out what God is doing. And how do we do that? Not by doing or saying anything but by listening.

3. 360-Degree Listening

As the name implies, 360-degree listening[13] means listening in all directions, three in particular—*up*, *in*, and *out*:

- *Up*: Listening to God
- *In*: Listening to people in our church and other churches
- *Out*: Listening to our community

Let's look at them in that order, though in practice, they are unlikely to happen quite that neatly.

Up: Listening to God

Some years ago, our church hall burned down. There were those who shrugged and said, "Well, let's take the insurance money and build a new one. No problem." But three leaders caught a different vision: a nonprofit housing complex on the site to serve the community. One, I am told, "would show up on [members'] doorsteps and plead his case for several hours." Finally, a majority of the congregation (though not all) agreed that this was what God was asking. The result was that in place of the old hall, the church built a low-rental apartment block with the resources of a church hall located in the basement. It was a brilliant solution. But the key was three people who saw beyond the obvious to what it might mean to be a gospel-shaped community in the neighborhood.

"What does God want for this church?" That is always the question for the church, in particular the church at a crossroads. After all, the gospel has brought the church into being, and Christians are those who have responded to the gospel in repentance and faith. It therefore makes perfect sense to ask, "How can our life as a Christian community best express the gospel in the world?"

So how do we figure out what God might be asking of us? Prayer is always a good place to begin. In every context where the church prays, we can ask, "Lord, help us discern what you are doing around here and what you are asking us to do" or "Lord, bless our neighbors and help this neighborhood flourish."

In: Listening to Our Church and Other Churches

From time to time, many churches will ask their members, "What part would you like to play in the Sunday service? Read Scripture, pray, sing in the choir, take up the offering?" Of course, there is nothing wrong with any of those: a worship service is a great context for various gifts of the body of Christ to be used.

But Christians also have gifts that can serve the mission of God outside the Sunday service. It's just that we tend to think about those rather less. But if we are seeking to be a "missional" church and "give away our life" for the gospel, why not do a survey of the congregation and ask a different kind of question? "What gifts do you have that might be used in ministry *outside* the church? Are you good at (for example) friendship, hospitality, speaking a second language, using the internet, finances, sports, working with children, baking, making connections between people?" These are all God-given missional skills—though (sadly) many Christians have never thought of them that way before.

Here's a lovely example I came across. Margaret is an older lady at a church in our neighborhood. Her church had recently been renovated, but when everyone else was celebrating, Margaret found herself wondering, "And now what? Are we just going to use this building for ourselves? What about the neighborhood? How can we open up to this community?" She began to think about what she could do and, in particular, the fact that she is a good knitter. Could God use that in outreach? Knitting as mission? Don't laugh.

With a little help, Margaret made posters and put them up around the community: apartment buildings (with the approval of the superintendents), the library, the local Starbucks, and the neighborhood association. She decided to put her phone number on the posters and began getting calls. Soon a small group of five or six came together. Margaret told me, "One lady joined because she was off work because of epilepsy. She had been in the city for five years and didn't really have anyone to connect with. She knits beautifully, and she came because of the notice in the library." Her last comment to me was fitting: "I love our group, and I trust God for the rest."[14]

One person with a simple gift offered to God and the mission of Jesus. Courage, skill, and love. A great combination. These things change the world.

Out: Listening to the Community

One church consultant friend of mine says, "You have to talk to the four *p*'s who know your community best: police, politicians, principals, and prostitutes." There may be local variations to this list, of course. For example, although the words don't begin with P, childcare agencies, community associations, community centers, EMS, and social services could easily be added to that list.

"But what do I say to them?" Well, a good start is to say, "We're from the church on the corner, and we are wondering whether there are some ways we can do a better job of contributing to the neighborhood. Do you mind if I ask you some questions?" What kind of questions? Nothing complicated or "religious" in any obvious sense. Questions like the following:

- What do you see happening in this neighborhood?

- How is the area changing?

- Is it becoming a better place to live or worse?

- What are the needs you are aware of?

- What causes you the most stress?

- What do you see bringing life to this neighborhood?

Apart from those general questions, you can also be more specific: Can you think of ways our church could serve this community? Are there times in the year when you need volunteers for a community project? For some, of course, even the fact that the questions are being asked by a church will be surprising.

One church planter friend asked his local councilor, "How could a new church serve this town?" It took the councilor a few minutes to understand the question. Then he said hesitantly, "Well, once a year, we have a campaign to clean up the town, and hardly anyone shows up." My friend smiled brightly: "We could help with that." The councilor looked puzzled. "But I thought the church was concerned about religious things?" That led to an interesting conversation, as you can imagine. The church obviously has an image problem.

You may be anxious about what kind of reception you will get. You don't usually have to worry. One friend, planting a church in a small town of forty thousand people, made an appointment to talk to the mayor. His secretary slotted her in for twenty minutes. One hour into the appointment, the church planter said, "Whoops, I'm taking much more time than you gave me. I should get out of here and let you get on." To which the mayor replied, "No, no, that's fine. I have never had a church leader come into my office and ask how they can serve the city before." Interesting.

People appreciate being listened to. And when they know we are listening, they will talk . . . and we may just hear the voice of God. Discuss what you are discovering with your church leadership and ask God for direction. Don't be afraid to start, and don't be afraid to make mistakes. Make haste slowly!

4. Look at Your Budget through a Mission Lens

What if you added a budget line to your church's budget and tagged it "for local outreach"? It doesn't have to be a huge amount at first. Begin with $100 or $250 or $500—whatever you can afford. Announce to the congregation that the money is available for outreach projects and that they should submit ideas. You will be amazed at the response.

One Presbyterian pastor told me this story. Penny was preaching about the story of the talents in Matthew 25. At the end of the sermon, she offered $40 to the congregation and invited people to think about taking it and investing it in kingdom work.

A few weeks later, she learned that one couple had taken one of the $20 bills and used the money to buy the ingredients for cookie making.[15] Then they invited another couple and their kids to their house to make cookies, which they then sold for $60. Their story was told to the church, and the $60 was then offered for reinvestment.

Another couple took that $60. They and some friends usually had lunch together at McDonald's after church. Now, instead, they invited the friends to their home for lunch, and each person put into the pot the amount they would have spent at McDonald's. The $60 thus grew to $185. More importantly, the group spent more than four hours together, talking and sharing in a way they had never done before. Other people in the group offered to host the group in the coming months.

As this story got around, others became involved with "reinvesting" until the total was almost $1,000. Meanwhile, Penny learned of a nearby home for women who were recently released from prison. The house needed a number of repairs, including new windows, for which they needed financial help. They were also trying to connect with the community. So the church decided to give them the money, which by now totaled around $1,500.

If your church had $1,500 not earmarked for any project, what would you do with it? Might you give it away like that? In kingdom terms, it was a wise investment.

5. Use the Church Building

What is your church building for? And who is it for? If it is a church building, then at its heart, its purpose is to serve the gospel, to be useful in serving God's mission in the world. Of course, it is also a gathering place for disciples of Jesus, a spiritual home for the Christian community. But the danger is that the first purpose—serving the gospel—can be overwhelmed by the second.

My friend Joe was a church planter in Sarnia, Ontario. He served on the committee of the annual arts festival, and at one meeting, they were discussing venues for the upcoming art exhibition. "Well," said Joe, "you would be very welcome to use our building."

"Ah," they responded, "but we would need to have it open Sunday morning, and that's when you do your church thing, right?"

Without missing a beat, Joe said, "Well, we would just skip our regular gathering that day and serve you coffee and cookies instead."

There was a collective gasp around the table, then the chair said, "Joe, you have just changed my whole view of church and Christianity." These things are radical, and they are noticed.

William Temple, once archbishop of Canterbury, said, "The church is the only society in the world that exists for the benefit of its non-members." The artists were nonmembers, so it was clear what the church had to do. This church remembered that they exist as part of God's mission to restore the whole world. They began to think and act "missionally."

6. Be Welcoming

A recent report on growing churches in Southern Ontario concluded that some churches were like peaches and others like coconuts. The peach churches were easy to get into: friendly and welcoming. And yet at the heart of them was something solid: a robust confidence in the gospel of Jesus and its power to change the world. And the coconuts? Well, you can guess. Hard on the outside, virtually impenetrable without a hammer or an ax. And if you finally succeeded in getting in, very little of substance was at the heart of them, and not worth the trouble.[16]

This is a large topic in itself, but let me summarize some of the things that contribute to our being a "peachy" church:[17]

- Before people ever come to our church, the likelihood is that they will look up our website. One new Christian told me, "I looked for a church website with pictures of the people: Were they friendly looking? Normal looking? Like me? When I found one, that's the church I went to." Frankly, you are not the best person to assess the friendliness of your website: ask a friend with no church connection to check it out. Who knows? If it's any good, they may even turn up on a Sunday.

- When they take the risk (and that's what it feels like) to come, who greets them and how? A stiff "Good morning" will not cut it. Only friendly and sensitive extroverts need apply.

- How easy is it to find their way through the service? Does someone at the front explain what is happening? Or how about inviting a newcomer to sit next to a member who can help them through the service? Putting everything in the bulletin can work too, of course, but the personal thing is nice.

- Is there a lot of "in-house" talk—sentences that begin "As you all know . . ." or "That Bible story so beloved of us all . . ." or "As Christians, we all rejoice that . . ."? Cut those out.

- What happens when the service ends? Does someone speak to visitors and invite them for coffee? You may say, "It's hard. I'm an introvert." For introverts (and I'm another of them), it requires what I can only call a naked act of the will—also known as obedience. Start by saying, "Hi. I don't think I've seen you here before. What brings you here this morning?" It's really not that difficult.

- Let's not assume that visitors are mature Christians new to the neighborhood and simply looking for a new church home. What if they are simply "exploring their spirituality," know nothing of Christian faith, and are wondering what church might offer them? Is there a place they can learn "the basics" of the gospel, Jesus, and the life of discipleship? Churches that are tuned in to this need will offer the Alpha course or a "Christianity 101,"[18] such as we discussed earlier, at least a couple of times a year.

A Presbyterian church consultant friend tells this story. He was doing a workshop on this exact topic of welcoming and at one point said, "I've visited four Presbyterian churches in recent weeks, and not one of them was welcoming."

In the break, a pastor came up to him and said, "I hope you will try our church soon. I think you'll find that it's different."

"Ah," said my friend, "yours was actually number three." Too often seeing ourselves as friendly means no more than that we are friendly to regular attendees, while we really have not the first idea how to approach new people.

The apostle Paul says, "Welcome one another, therefore, just as Christ has welcomed you, for the glory of God" (Rom 15:7). You may remember my suggestion that the glory of God is what God is really like, a glimpse of the true nature of God.[19] So what is God like? One thing the gospel shows is that God is a welcoming

God—welcoming prodigals home but also welcoming back a world that has gone astray. So Paul understands that when we welcome strangers, at the church door or any other time, we are giving them a taste of the welcome of God. Let's never underestimate the power of genuine welcome. It's not just a job; it's a sacrament, and greeters are its administrators.

THINGS TO BEWARE

When we begin to think "mission," there are a few automatic reactions that at first sight look good but can easily work against real mission.

Starting a New Worship Service

"What could possibly be wrong with a new service—contemporary, informal, and welcoming?" you may ask. After all, we know about worship, we do it well, and it's a way people can encounter God. It's also what our ordained leaders are trained to do.

Frankly, the fact that it is familiar to us should itself raise warning flags. Things that are easy and comfortable to us may well be alien and off-putting to those who do not share our faith. This is why research in the community is so important. If it turns out that what people outside the church are asking for is a new worship service, then by all means, let's do that—and consult them about what shape it should take. But nonchurched people are very unlikely to be asking for a new service.

Starting Something inside the Existing Church Building

"Let's do a weekly coffeehouse in the church basement!" Again, we need to ask, Why are we thinking of using the church building? The answer is likely to be, well, that it doesn't cost anything, we know our way around, and it's like a second home to us.

The problem is the same as that of the worship service: the church building may be a comfortable place for us, but by the same token, it may be a very uncomfortable place for our friends. It certainly doesn't feel like any kind of home. I heard of one woman who wanted to try church for the first time. Three Sundays in a row, she got as far as the main door of the church, then turned around and went home as quickly as she could. When it came to the point, the prospect was just too threatening.

Appointing a Staff Member for Mission and Outreach

It makes perfect sense, doesn't it? If you think something is important in church life and you can afford it, then employ an expert (preferably trained) to lead that ministry. That's why we have (depending on our tradition) youth leaders, worship leaders, children's ministry leaders, seniors' ministry leaders, and so on. If we think mission and outreach are important, appoint someone to head it up. Surely that will make it happen, right?

"Head it up": aye, there's the rub. This may not be a problem for (say) children's ministry, but the problem with a minister of outreach (or whatever we call them) is that it is all too easy for us then to heave a sigh of relief and say, "Wow, isn't that great? Now that's looked after. While he or she brings in all the new people, let's get back to the real problem of the quality of the toilet paper in the washrooms."

You see my point, I'm sure. This makes mission an add-on (or, as the Brits say, a "bolt-on") to "normal" church life. One such staff member recalls that the church "honestly believed that I would just walk out into one of the most hostile-to-the-gospel neighborhoods and bring people into this unwelcoming, faith-is-for-Sunday-only setting." Perhaps more significantly, he reflected later, "From very early on, I realized that my job needed to shift its focus to congregational formation. Almost no one in the congregation was ready for evangelism. The ethos of the entire church needed to change."

The key to congregational formation, I don't need to tell you by now, is the gospel of Jesus Christ and its outworking in lives of discipleship. Of course, when that is the case, a staff member may be helpful to lead and direct the work—but the danger is that we will expect such a person to do it all. And that can be disastrous.

Grabbing an Off-the-Shelf Program

"Any port in a storm," some people say, meaning that if you are in a crisis, you will grab the help that's closest to hand. And—in the case of mission anyway—the closest to hand may not actually be the most helpful in the long run.

Case in point: Do you know about Messy Church? It's a wonderful outreach program for nonchurched families. It involves crafts, music, celebration, disciple making . . . and food.[20] What's not to like? Many inherited churches hear about Messy Church and think, "Wow, we need young families in this church, so we'll start Messy Church." But it may not work. Why? Because it short-circuits the process of 360-degree listening.

I don't want to boast, but my own church started Messy Church seven years ago. That decision came out of a six-month listening program that we undertook in conjunction with a neighboring church of a different tradition. Among other findings, we discovered that young families were asking for places in the neighborhood where they could gather with other young families. Well, that's certainly one of the things Messy Church does. So we launched it, and it went well. One early highlight was when one mother reported that "Messy Church is the talk of the school playground!" High praise indeed.

Well, you see my point. Off-the-shelf programs could be right for our church. But we shouldn't rush into adopting them too quickly. Take whatever time it takes to do the listening first.

WHAT DO YOU WANT ME TO DO FOR YOU?

All this that I have described is a process that might take six months or more before you decide what God is calling you to do. That might feel like a long time, but frankly it is better than rushing into something just because you want to get on with it. The danger then is that things don't work out because it wasn't really the right thing, and that leaves people with a bad taste that can linger for years.

Jesus's question to the blind man (Mark 10:51)—"What do you want me to do for you?"—often puzzles people. He's talking to a man who is blind. Isn't it obvious what he wants? Apparently not.

When churches are in decline, it seems obvious what they need: they need revitalization. But is that really what they want? More than one young pastor has been hired because he and the congregation agree that what they need is "change." But six months later, it has become obvious that what the pastor and the people mean by change is completely different, and the two go their separate ways.

This chapter has been written on the assumption that declining churches really mean it when they say they want change. I hope I'm right.

CHAPTER 9

THE GOSPEL AND CHURCH PLANTING
Two Models

"Start a new church? Why on earth would you do that when there are so many empty churches that need filling up?" It sounds logical enough, doesn't it, but it reflects a common misunderstanding. One assumption is that churches are meant to last forever. Well, some may, but most don't. Another is that there are ready-made Christian communities that can simply be transported lock, stock, and barrel across town to where there happens to be an empty church building for them to take over. There may be circumstances where this happens, but it is the exception, not the rule.

Here's a different way of approaching the question. A friend of mine says, "Churches are like people: every day some die and others are born." The area where I live, where many homes were built in the first part of the twentieth century, used to have a lot of beautiful mature trees. Over the years, however, one after another they have died and been cut down. The number on our street is already less than half what it was when we moved into the neighborhood some twenty years ago. I was lamenting this loss to the local tree expert one day, and he shrugged and said, "I've been telling the city this would happen for years. I've advised them to start planting new trees before the old ones have all gone. But," he added with a touch of bitterness, "the city always has more important priorities."

It will not surprise you by now that I want to start by considering what church planting has to do with the gospel. Neither will it surprise you to know that I think the gospel and church planting are closely related. To put it another way, if we understand the gospel, we will want to plant new churches. It's as simple as that.

Here is how it follows from everything else I have said so far:

- The gospel speaks of God's determination to remove sin and evil from the world and to make all things new through Jesus Christ.

- This good news is for the whole world that God made.

- The primary vehicle by which that restoring love is to be communicated to the world is the church, where the gospel of Jesus is central: it is understood and experienced, celebrated and lived out.

- The gospel will be expressed differently (in the way we talk and the way we live) in different cultures.

- Where there are places that have neither experienced the love of God nor heard it explained, the church needs to go there, to live and teach the gospel.

- The result of such witness will be new churches— communities of Jesus's apprentices—in those places.

One way to test this theory is to count how many people in new churches ask for baptism. This is not an infallible guide to healthy church growth. However, for an adult to be baptized means (presumably) that they never heard or responded to the gospel before. And in fact, churches that keep a tally of such baptisms do see a significantly higher number in new churches than in old. Among the Southern Baptists, for example, "established . . . churches report 3.4 baptisms per 100 resident members [each year], whereas new churches average 11.7."[1] That's a huge difference.

If we care about Jesus's good news, therefore, we will be concerned for church planting. You can't have one without the other. That's easy to say, however. What does it look like in Western cultures these days?

There are different models of church planting across the world today. I am going to describe two models of how this is being done, at opposite ends of a spectrum. In reality, however, there are many models in between, combining elements of the two extremes in different ways and different proportions.[2] I am tempted to say that the principles that inform the second model are the way of the future in an increasingly secularized Western world, but I am open to being persuaded otherwise. Slightly open, anyway.

First, then, let's discuss what I would call the traditional model of church planting.

TRADITIONAL CHURCH PLANTING:
IF YOU BUILD IT, THEY WILL COME

At the risk of caricaturing this approach, it means buying a piece of land in a new subdivision, putting up an A-frame church building, appointing a full-time pastor, and putting out a sign advertising service times with the hope that "if you build it, they will come." That might seem like a rather demeaning parody. Having talked to people who have planted churches that way, however, I know that it was (and is) a demanding, deeply self-sacrificial, and even heroic method. And in many instances, the strategy has been successful, though not as universally as it once was.

The world has changed since the day when this was the unquestioned method, however. A few years back, I asked my friend Reg Stackhouse, who planted an Anglican church, St. Matthew's, Islington (Toronto), in the 1950s, to reflect on his experience and how things have changed.

He told of a time when the only visible sign of a church was "a vacant lot and a sign proclaiming, 'An Anglican Church Will Be Built Here!'" He talked about how he cycled from street to street in the new subdivisions and invited people (often newly arrived from Britain) to come to the fledgling church, which began worship in the basement of the unfinished church. Many in those days already had a degree of experience in church in their background, and many were trying to find community, so the church was a great place to gather and meet others. Reg commented that they had baptisms of children every month, as many young families joined the church.

The rate of expansion did not last, however. He reflected, "We expected the future to continue to unfold in just the same way as we had seen in the previous few years." But immigration from the UK, which had fueled the growth, declined around 1965, and as a result, so did the church. "During the second half of the twentieth century," Reg lamented, "we failed to grapple with the need for another really fresh expression of church."[3]

If that was true in the 1960s, it is even more so now. In Western countries such as the United States and Canada, where the number of those with no religious affiliation and no church background grows with each passing year, especially among the young,[4] it is more often the case that "if you build it," they will not come; they will neither notice nor care.

In other cases, church planting by visible minorities is often successful when using traditional "gathering" strategies. The dynamic is easy to understand. Suppose you are freshly arrived from, let us say, Korea, and everything in your new environment is unfamiliar, from the language to the food to the architecture. After a few days, you meet a fellow Korean, and the immediate pleasure and sheer relief at meeting someone who understands what you are going through is huge. Then your new friend says, "Hey, you should come with me on Sunday morning. At my church, we're all Korean. The service is in Korean, the food after the service is Korean, and the singles group is full of great people." Are you going to go? You bet you are. And the fact that it is a church is, frankly, of secondary interest—at least at the beginning.

The other exception to the rule that new churches do not automatically attract new people is when a neighborhood has a high proportion of dechurched people: people who have had a meaningful church connection in the past but for one reason or another have moved away from it. In that case, a lively new church in a traditional building with relatively familiar services may be very attractive, not least to young families who would like their children to have the kind of church experience the parents once had. The leader of one such church plant was upfront about his goal: "We aim to engage mostly with dechurched people in our neighborhood . . . who mostly haven't been engaged in a church for the past several years."[5]

But this is a "shrinking window."[6] In the next twenty years in Western cultures, the dechurched are going to be almost completely replaced by the nonchurched, for whom traditional church "is a foreign land."[7]

There, then, is the first model of church planting. The strengths and weaknesses of it are obvious. The other end of the spectrum of approaches to church planting is what we can call "contextual church planting."

CONTEXTUAL CHURCH PLANTING

The phrase "foreign land" is a reminder of what we have said already about culture and adaptation. All too often, traditional church is completely alien to the culture around it. There are increasing numbers of people who are never going to turn up at our churches on a Sunday morning, however warm and welcoming those churches may be. It is simply too much of a cultural jump for them.

The problem is not the gospel itself—though that is problematic in its own way, with its focus on the cross and its challenge to our sinful autonomy—but our own cultural "stuff" with which we have surrounded the gospel. The water is what is important, not our preferred container. And that container may make the water inaccessible. Here is Newbigin's warning, issued some forty years ago: "It is not enough in this situation for the Church to say 'Come—all are welcome.' A few may accept the invitation, but only to become assimilated to the language, culture, and style of the already existing congregation."[8]

This is why visible minority churches, or traditional churches that attract the dechurched, are effective. There are no cultural barriers to an encounter with the gospel. There is no cultural interference to mess with the reception of the radio signal.

What then of the rest of the population, with its rapidly growing proportion of the nonchurched? This is where our theology of culture fits in.

If the nonchurched are to hear the good news of the kingdom and have the opportunity to become apprentices of Jesus, then the church will have to go where they are, not wait for them to come to us. And the churches that emerge in those places where the church has never been before may look very different from those we're used to. In fact, I can readily think of four new churches whose denominations are not quite sure what to make of them: "They don't look like other churches of our denomination. What do we make of them? Are they really churches? And how do we respond to them?" This is why these new communities are sometimes called "fresh expressions of church" or "worshipping communities"—carefully avoiding the bold and controversial claim that they are simply "churches."[9]

How does this kind of church planting differ from the traditional model? In many cases, church planting in a post-Christendom world is more likely to arise from the grass roots, seeded by Christian involvement in a particular community. One young Canadian church planter told me, "We're not setting out to plant churches. We're just setting out to be witnesses to the gospel. But where the gospel takes root through that witness, new churches will be the result." That is wisdom.

One might ask, Where people begin to respond to the gospel, why can they not simply get involved in existing churches and maybe help revive them? The answers are sad but not hard to find. Not infrequently, the problem is the existing church, which is unwilling to be flexible in order to accommodate the new believers—which is rather like a family that refuses to change its way of doing things in order to accommodate the needs of a newborn baby. It is also true, however, that those churches' buildings are often in the wrong place to influence a neighborhood where the gospel is not known. They were built to serve a particular population, but the population has moved.

In any case, there is an argument to be made that new churches multiply the diversity within the body of Christ—which is a good thing. In theological terms, the diversity more clearly displays the many-faceted glory of God. Newbigin even echoes the words of Revelation 21:26 about "the glory and the honor of the nations" being brought into the New Jerusalem: "Those who are left outside [existing churches] have their treasures to bring into the Holy City—their own treasures, not borrowings from others."[10]

On a pragmatic level, this kind of culturally based planting enables the church to reach out to more and more diverse populations who would otherwise never hear the good news. Newbigin anticipates this: "We ought to expect that there is brought to birth . . . outside the walls of the church as it is now, a community which is the first-fruit of the gospel in that place. It should have its own proper character as distinct from that of the community from which the mission came."[11] In other words, it will be a new Christian community that reflects the culture of the neighborhood around it and not that of the "mother" church that gave it birth.

So how do new churches begin today if not with a building and a paid pastor? There is a methodology emerging among young church planters. Having said that, I do wonder if *methodology* is not too fancy a word for what is often simply an intuitive strategy. This approach begins with prayer, not a program; not with a building but with relationships; with offering service rather than leading services; and with discerning where God is already at work rather than with a predetermined strategy. Often these new ventures are led by laypeople with little or no formal theological education. Not infrequently, those who begin them are bivocational—working at a part-time job in order to support their church planting. And many of these new communities will not be recognizably "church-like" in the early stages—and those stages may last several years.

Bishop Steve Croft offers what I think is the clearest definition: these new worshipping communities, or fresh expressions of church, he suggests, are the fruit of "the attempt to go to where people are, listen carefully to the context, and through service form new communities of faith which have the potential to grow into church in their own right."[12] There are five stages in that definition, not always as clearly distinguishable as the wording might suggest:

1. "Go to *where people are* . . ."

    Instead of waiting for people to come to us or organizing programs that might attract them, the church goes to where they are. One church planter said, slightly tongue in cheek, "I guess the church began when my family and I moved into the neighborhood."

2. *"listen carefully to the context . . ."*

This refers to the "360-degree listening" discussed in the previous chapter. We get to know people by hanging out with them on the streets and in coffee shops, waiting for kids at the end of the school day, and standing in line at the supermarket. What are they talking about? What are their hopes, their fears, their needs? Some of this listening may be more systematic, with questionnaires and surveys. Those are not intrinsically unspiritual and may uncover realities that casual personal conversations cannot.

3. *"through service . . ."*

How might the good news of Jesus be expressed practically in this place? I think of three contextual church plants and how they serve. In one case, the church began with a storefront bicycle repair shop where local young people learned practical skills. In another, the "mother church" sponsored a restaurant in a poorer part of the city, and it then grew into a church. In the third instance, the founders set up a used bookstore with a coffee shop attached.[13]

Now a health warning: do not try these specific approaches in your neighborhood. ("Let's start a used bookstore!") These are not cookie-cutter programs that can simply be reproduced anywhere. It is not "the answer" for a church to do any of these things. In every case, they are the fruit of "going" and "listening carefully." They grew from the grassroots up, and were not imposed top-down by someone in the church or a denominational office that just had a neat idea they had seen working somewhere else. They are incarnational, in the best sense of the word.

4. *"form new communities of faith . . ."*

Loving service creates relationships of trust, and in such relationships, important things, such as faith, can be discussed. Sometimes this may lead to a "discussion group to learn about Jesus." Sometimes the Alpha program may be appropriate. And in other contexts, a simple worship service may be the right thing to do. You may ask, How do you decide? My answer will be unhelpful, I know, but it's the only realistic one: it all depends—on the context, the neighborhood, the community, the people. But you probably figured I was going to say that.

5. *"which have the potential to grow into church in their own right."*

So is this now a church? I would argue that churches are like people: when they are at the embryonic stage, it takes some imagination to envision what the adult will look like. This is why Rowan Williams, when asked whether a particular fresh expression of church was "really" a church, replied, "Let's wait and see." All being well, yes, this new community of faith will grow in time to have the recognizable marks of a mature church, such as discussed in chapter 5. But in the meantime, let's not criticize the embryo—or in some cases the adolescent!— for not being an adult. Instead, let's pray and do whatever we can to help them grow to maturity.

Enough of the theoretical stuff. What does all this look like on the ground—in real neighborhoods? Every new worshipping community, every fresh expression of church, will be different, because every neighborhood—and ultimately every individual within that neighborhood—is different. So it is generally counterproductive to try to reproduce something done in a particular community. Here is Newbigin again: "The character of the [new] local church will not be determined primarily by the character, tastes, dispositions, etc., of its members, but by those of the secular society in which and for which it lives—seen in the light of God's redemptive purpose revealed in Jesus Christ for all."[14]

However, there are some principles underlying all these pioneering efforts, and the best way to learn them is to observe a fresh expression of church in action and then reflect. Time for a story.

My friend Matt was associate pastor at an evangelical church in a community fifteen minutes' drive down the highway from his home in Hamilton (Ontario). Over time, he came to realize that other church members who lived in his area were making the same commute Sunday after Sunday. They began to wonder whether perhaps they should be "being church" in their own neighborhood instead of commuting to a place where they had few connections other than the friends they saw on Sundays and other church gatherings.

What to do? They began to meet for prayer on a Wednesday evening monthly while still attending the "mother church" on Sundays. (Later, they increased the frequency to weekly, which raised the commitment bar significantly.) This lasted eighteen months. During that time, they also began to explore their neighborhood, to try to discover where God was at work and where they might be the presence of Christ.

At this point, most churches would start a Sunday worship service and advertise a big "launch," hoping to persuade the neighbors to attend. The St. Clair community—at some point it was decided to name it for one of the streets running through the neighborhood—did indeed start a worship service, but there was no "launch" and no advertising. The service was mainly for the planting team and any friends they might choose to invite, but they kept it low-key. Matt told me, with a twinkle in his eye, "We didn't even have PowerPoint!" They put no emphasis on getting members to invite people. They were planting a church, not a Sunday service.

For that reason, from the start, they emphasized the centrality of local groups on various streets within the neighborhood. These groups were called "missional families," which emphasized the two key aspects of their identity: they were groups of families, and they were called to God's mission. Their job was (and still is) to gather weekly for a meal, for sharing, for discussing last Sunday's sermon, and for discussing how best to serve the neighborhood. They also invited neighbors to come and enjoy food, friendship, and lively discussion. This is the heartbeat of the church.

As a result, on some Sundays, the St. Clair community does not meet for corporate worship but meets instead in missional families. That's how important mission in the neighborhood is: it can even take precedence over Sunday worship. Behind this is the realization that Sunday morning cannot do everything that is needed to form disciples for mission. To try to make it do so is to ask more of it than it is capable of delivering, which comes close to a definition of idolatry: expecting what is basically a good gift of God to do more than it is capable of doing.[15]

So how do they serve their neighborhood? Early on, church members visited the local school to ask if there was some way they could be helpful. One answer was that they could provide backpacks for the start of the school year. They did that—and baked muffins for the teachers.

Soon after the weekly praying began, Matt ran into the local city councilor, who asked what Matt hoped for in starting a church. I don't know what kind of answer he expected—"To grow the church to a thousand every Sunday," perhaps. Matt's answer was rather different: "To make disciples of Jesus and to make this a better place to live." They were friends from that moment on. And when the councilor came across needs in the community that were not being met by regular services, he would call Matt: "Can you guys help?" Once it was an elderly lady whose basement had flooded and who couldn't afford to get it fixed. Another time, it was a resident who had been shot at and needed to relocate at short notice.

The councilor recently decided not to run for reelection, and the connection seemed in danger of coming to an end. But then the outgoing councilor called Matt to say, "I want to arrange a coffee where I can introduce you to my successor." In other words, St. Clair has come to be a valued partner with those serving the larger community—not shut away in a religious ghetto but living the life of Christ out in their world. The future looks promising.

PRINCIPLES

Many of the ideas practiced at St. Clair are applicable elsewhere, even though the specifics are not. Here are some of those I observe, which I have seen implemented in different ways, though with equal effectiveness:

1. *They don't care much about size.*

"Small is beautiful" was a slogan of the 1970s, but it remains an apt summary of the attitude of many new churches, including St. Clair.[16] Randy is a church planter friend on the West coast who had grown a church of one thousand people. One Sunday, he got up to preach. The lights dimmed and the spotlight came on him. And he suddenly thought to himself, "What kind of church is this, where I can't see the faces of the people I'm preaching to?" This triggered what he described later as "an ecclesiological crisis," which led to his resignation a few months afterward. This was followed by a year's sabbatical, and then a second attempt to start a church—this time of a size where he could see people's faces. Such considerations are not trivial or negligible to today's church planters. They are basic. Size works against relationships.

2. *They don't necessarily start with a worship service.*

Many, perhaps most, traditional church plants start with Sunday worship. After all, that is when church is most visible, and it is often what trained church leaders do best. So how do we know we are church? When we do Sunday worship and when we have a lot of people present (if necessary, bussed in from elsewhere to boost the numbers).

In a post-Christendom society, however, this is seldom the best approach.

Why on earth would that be the case? It seems very counter-intuitive. Well, once you start worship, there are at least three dangers. One is that the preparation for Sunday will begin to take up a significant proportion of your time during the week. Another is that you will become a magnet for Christians from all over your town or city who are looking for the newest, coolest church in town but who are unlikely to care about your neighborhood or your vision for it.[17] Last, and perhaps most important, those outside the church with whom you are becoming connected may well not be ready for Sunday services. One promising church plant I know of fell apart because the sponsoring denomination insisted after a certain length of time that the planters begin Sunday worship—in a church building outside the immediate neighborhood—prematurely. The community with whom the planters were sharing life was not ready for that, and as a result, the whole thing disintegrated.

3. *They don't emphasize the building.*

St. Clair will need a building soon because they are outgrowing the restaurant where they have met since the beginning. But like many new churches, they sit light to the idea of owning a building. And as they look at various possibilities, one key question is, Will this building enhance or restrict our present ministries? Most traditional churches simply accept that they cannot do certain things because of the shape, size, and location of their buildings. A new church has the unique possibility of putting ministries first and buildings second.

4. *They stress neighborhood ministry.*

I wonder what the word *parish* means to you. Traditionally, it meant the geographical area around a church building that the church regarded as the area for which it was spiritually responsible, whether or not the local people attended worship. In some areas, this meaning continues, but in many contexts, the meaning has shrunk to mean "the people who show up for worship on a Sunday"—who may or may not be from the neighborhood.

New worshipping communities are rediscovering the importance of place and reclaiming the notion of "parish."[18] St. Clair exists *in* the Sherman neighborhood of Hamilton *for* the Sherman neighborhood. The majority of the members, including the staff, live in the neighborhood, and the "missional families" seek to serve the people around them. It is incarnational gospel ministry.

5. They relate more to local networks than to denominational structures.

Not every historic denomination understands the dynamics of contextual church planting. In many cases, the most useful support comes instead from others in the local Christian community who know the context and share the vision.

Recently, I came across a lovely example of respecting local realities. A pastor shared with me that his church felt ready to plant. (His present church was itself a plant not so many years ago: thinking this way is obviously in their DNA.) One of the first things the church did was to get a map of the city where they were located, mark every existing church on the map, and then identify an area with no churches around. That is where they are going to plant. What a wise and gracious strategy! Not only does this avoid the danger of competition with other churches (which seems to me an abomination); it also prioritizes taking the gospel to a place where (we assume) the good news of Jesus is not yet known or experienced—which is the number one reason for starting new churches.

6. Their small groups are missional.

I know the word *missional* is a slippery one. But it's really not that complicated: missional simply means being committed to the mission of God as expressed in the gospel.

How does this affect small groups? Most churches have small groups, which exist for fellowship, prayer, and Bible study. All good things, of course. But the problem can be expressed quite simply: the calling of the gospel is to turn outward; the tendency of sinful human beings is to turn inward. And small groups all too often ignore the first and fall into the trap of the second.

So if small groups in a church plant want to stay missional, they will have mission in their DNA from day one. They will come together not just to support one another but to support one another in mission. One way to do this is for groups to be formed on the basis of neighborhoods, as at St. Clair. This means there is a physical reminder of mission every day, as group members go to work and do their shopping and interact with neighbors.

Other groups may come into being to work together in a particular missional activity—visiting in a local prison, for example, or helping out with a ministry to disadvantaged youth. There is still the danger that groups will turn inward, of course—that's human nature—but it is easier to recall people to what they initially committed to than to introduce new DNA to the culture.

TRADITIONAL AND CONTEXTUAL

What follows is an oversimplification, as diagrams like this tend to be. But I still think it is quite helpful to contrast traditional and contextual church plants by portraying them in black-and-white terms, like this.

CHURCH PLANT TYPE	TRADITIONAL	CONTEXTUAL
Focus	Building centered. Church has not really started until the building is secured.	Community centered. Being church does not depend on a building, so finding one is secondary.
Priority activity	Getting worship started. The date for the launch is usually set well in advance.	Relationships and service. Worship will begin when the community is ready.
Basic philosophy	Attractional, centripetal, "Come to us."	Integration, centrifugal, "We'll come to you."
Attitude to location	The neighborhood is of secondary significance. Most people drive to church, so it's not that important.	The neighborhood is fundamental. Most people walk (or bike) to church and are involved in the life of the area.

(continued)

(table continued)

CHURCH PLANT TYPE	TRADITIONAL	CONTEXTUAL
Membership	A critical mass of Christians at worship is crucial, sometimes "imported" to "bulk up" the numbers, at least at the beginning.	The emphasis is on Christians already in the neighborhood; visitors from other areas are encouraged to find a church closer to home.
Models	May follow a model used by other church plants. Following the recipe more or less guarantees results.	Unique to context. It is impossible to tell what the mature church will look like.
Evangelism	Emphasis on evangelism through Sunday worship and programs like Alpha.	Emphasis on evangelism through relationships and small groups.
Small groups	Fellowship-oriented.	Serving missionally in the neighborhood.

It's obvious, I know, that I have a preference. I only hope I have represented traditional church plants fairly, because it is an ongoing cause of distress to me that God does not always think as I do. I sometimes have the sense that God is listening to my wonderful ideas and is saying gently, "Thank you, John. That's just lovely. I really like your diagram. But actually, I am going to do what I am going to do. And I'm sorry, but it may not fit with your ideas."

So there may be traditional church plants that thrive and flourish. There are certainly church plants that combine aspects of the old approach and the new—starting with a building but simultaneously engaging the neighborhood, for example. There are all sorts of permutations. I'm just telling you my preference and why it is my preference in light of the gospel. But God is God. I have learned that the hard way.

WHO IS A CHURCH PLANTER?

Church planting, then, is an important expression of the gospel. If we understand the good news of God's work in the world through Christ, we will understand the need for a community that witnesses to the gospel by life and word in every neighborhood.

But who can plant a new church? Obviously, not everybody. Not even every pastor. Not everybody with seminary training (and that includes me). There are particular kinds of leadership that a post-Christendom, missional situation requires. And that is sufficiently important to require a chapter all to itself.

THE GOSPEL AND LEADERSHIP
The Many and the Few

If there is one topic that dominates the thinking of church leadership these days, it is . . . *church leadership*. Books, blogs, seminars, consultancies, and conferences are full of the topic. Their number seems to have increased as the decline of the church in the West has accelerated. Maybe we think leadership is the magic bullet that will restore the church's fortunes.

The New Testament, however, doesn't seem very interested in "leadership," in spite of the church's gospel-powered growth. Jesus uses the word *leader* only once (Luke 22:26), and even then his comment is negative. When the word is used elsewhere in the Gospels, it is not used of the disciples. It is always "a leader of the synagogue," "a leader of the Pharisees," or "a leader of the people." And though Paul does include it in his lists of gifts of the Spirit, leadership is mentioned almost last.[1]

So is leadership really that important? Should we be spending all this time and effort on it? And—this is my concern—how does the subject relate to the theme of a Christianity and a church that is shaped by the gospel? Here, I think, is the connection: good leadership is one of the most significant keys in the church's becoming a gospel-centered community. But we have to understand what Christian leadership is and (equally important) what it is not.

ONLY LARRY CAN BE LARRY

One thing that shaped my own understanding of leadership was working with a leadership program for teens at a summer camp. What on earth did it mean for all sixty of those sixteen- and seventeen-year-olds to become "leaders"? We used to address this early in the program. I would invite Larry to come to the session as Exhibit A. Larry was six foot six and directed the boys' camp across the lake. He had a booming voice and could hold a dining room of 150 unruly young boys spellbound with his storytelling. Everyone loved and admired Larry. He was a real Leader, with a capital L.

So I would stand Larry in front of the teens and tell them that this was what the program would turn them into. Some of them would have to grow significantly taller. (They had been told the program would stretch them, but not how.) Some were the wrong gender. A voice coach would help them develop that loud, booming voice. Most would have to develop significantly in that fruit of the Spirit known as "chutzpah." But the program would help them in all these areas.

By now it was clear this was not intended seriously. But the lesson was obvious: Larry was the kind of leader that only he could be. He led in a way that used all of his natural God-given attributes, and it was a wonder to behold. But nobody else could be Larry. In that case, what kind of leader could others be? Well, by the same token, the kind of leader that God made them to be. If they were leading four kids in their tent, or a canoeing class at the waterfront, or an overnight hiking trip, they would do it in a way that was recognizably theirs. There were things they could learn from leaders like Larry, of course, as I myself have, but the way they led would be an expression of their God-given attributes and no one else's.

So often the things we teach to others come home to roost in our own hearts. Not only were these teenagers not Larry; I wasn't Larry either. And though Larry and I love and respect each other, my gifts and abilities are very different from his. Don't ask me to bring order to 150 lively small boys with a single word. I shudder at the thought of trying. But on the other hand, I have debated philosophy professors on the existence of God in front of hundreds of university students, something Larry has never done and never could do, as he will cheerfully tell you.

This has led to a deep-seated conviction about the nature of leadership in the church: we lead according to who God has made us. Or, to put it another way, we lead in the areas where we are gifted.

Some time ago, I was at a meeting of church leaders in my city. One person, Sue, is a highly respected spiritual director who gives direction to several of the senior leaders. When it was her turn to introduce herself, she began by saying, "I don't know why I'm here. I'm really not a leader." Everybody around the table laughed, though with great affection. No, Sue is not a preacher, or a church planter, or a denominational executive, or anything else that we often mean by "leader." But when she exercises her gifts of spiritual direction, people sit up and take notice. That's where and how she leads.

And this is true for all of us. If I had a gift for flower arranging (and I don't), it is conceivable that, by a natural process, I might become the leader of the flower arranging team. If not, someone more gifted at it than me would become the leader. It needs to be underlined, however, that the opposite is also true: we will never be very effective at leading in areas where we are not gifted. We may be able to do it for a time (I speak from experience), but it's better to avoid ever doing it if you can.

Maybe this complexity is one reason the New Testament doesn't bother too much with the word *leader*. The reality of leadership is more varied than any single term implies. But what the New Testament does talk about is spiritual gifts. There are five lists of gifts in the New Testament, all different, though with some overlap.[2] If you add up all the gifts, there are more than thirty. But Michael Green's view is typical of how scholars interpret this topic: "All these lists are seeking to give samples of what the Spirit will do in the life of the believer, not to make exhaustive lists of gifts."[3]

I suspect the other reason the New Testament isn't terribly interested in "leadership" is because it conjures up so many images that are inimical to what Jesus was about. Not surprisingly, therefore, the one time he uses the word, he explicitly subverts such images. The First Nations Version expresses it powerfully. Jesus has just warned that someone will betray him:

> This led to an argument about which one of them was to be seen as the first and greatest among them. So Creator Sets Free [Jesus] reminded them, "Rulers from the Nations show their power by forcing people around, and then call it 'helping them.' This will not be the way of the ones who walk my road. The greatest among you will be least, like a child, and the rulers will be like household servants. Who is the greater one?" he asked, "The one who is being served or the one who serves? Is it not the one being served?" he responded. "But here I am serving you." (Luke 22:24–27 FNV)

This was also helpful in teaching teenagers about leadership. In the Christian world, to lead is to serve. You want to be a great leader? Learn to be a great servant. I told them that on four separate occasions I had come across camp directors cleaning the toilets in their camps, not "to set an example," but just because it needed doing. Setting up for meals, washing dishes, and keeping the waterfront clean, which the young leaders they did every day, were not irrelevant to the training: they were central to the training. And the "leaders" of the program, naturally, took the lead in such tasks. Unless all of us learned to be content doing such things, we would never be considered leaders in Jesus's eyes.

As I reflect on this topic of leadership and giftedness, my mind moves to the question of how the gospel interacts with all our gifts, whatever they are. Three things strike me in particular.

1. Servant leaders are being shaped by the gospel.

Whatever gifts people have, their leadership in those areas is dependent on their grasp of the gospel—or, better, how far they are being grasped by the gospel. Leaders are those who live, move, and have their being in the context of God's renewal of all things. It is their environment, as water is a fish's environment. They have heard Jesus's good news about God, and they have responded by giving up their own self-directed lives. They have given their lives instead to following Jesus, to play their part in the work of the gospel. In traditional language, they have repented and believed. In a word, they are disciples. That's basic.

Discipleship happens on two levels. It doesn't only shape what I do in the world (though it will do that); it also shapes who I am. It is not just the world "out there" that is in need of renewal; it is also me and my internal world. Both are included in God's plan. As I said earlier, the two have to go together.

Leaders in the secular world have no such constraints. If I am CEO of the Cancer Society, my worldview hardly matters as long as I do a good job. Just because I own a coffee shop, it doesn't mean I love coffee. Even if I head up an ethical investment firm, there is no guarantee that I am myself ethical. I just need good business skills.

Not so in the church. In the church, whether my servant/leader role is as pastor, small group leader, janitor, or flower arranger, I cannot encourage others to follow Christ unless I myself am following Christ. This is why Peter urges elders to pastor by example (1 Pet 5:1–2). This is not just a matter of integrity, though it certainly is that. It is also the case that, unless I am seriously following Christ, I will actually lead people astray. Unless I am allowing Jesus by his Spirit to work on my pride, my impatience, my lack of love, or my fear of change (to take some random examples), there will be trouble—quite apart from the normal troubles that will occur in any community.

2. Servant leaders enable churches to engage with the gospel.

Leadership may have any one of a thousand goals. The leader of a political party hopes to lead her party to power. The leader of a hiking expedition hopes everybody will have an enjoyable and safe time. It's obvious, isn't it?

So what is the goal of leadership in the church? As with everything else in the church, our gifts and abilities exist to serve Jesus and his gospel, the good news of God's coming kingdom. The church came into existence in the first place in response to that good news, and Jesus has commissioned his church to spread that good news by word and deed. That's the name of the game.

The primary job of every Christian servant, then, whatever their gifts, is to help the church be the church. As simple as that.

For example, let's start with those whose responsibility has to do with the gathered community and the place where it meets. (We know this is not the only expression of church, but it's the easiest to identify.) Janitors don't just look after the building. Think of it this way. They are creating a place where the body of Christ can gather in (relative) comfort to be equipped for the work of the gospel. The community can concentrate better on that task if the heating and lighting are working, if rain is not dripping from the ceiling, if everything is clean, and if there is enough toilet paper. (I am not joking.)

Is the janitor a servant, enabling the body? Of course. Is the janitor a leader? Well, if you have ever crossed a janitor, you know the answer. If you are smart, you will recognize and submit to the janitor's authority and expertise in the areas where he or she serves.

The same may be said of treasurers, secretaries, greeters, worship leaders, A/V teams, webmasters, and coffeemakers. And yes, I almost forgot the flower arrangers. They create an environment conducive to worshipping God, thereby reminding us of the story we live by, allowing us to learn more about being apprentices of Jesus, and encouraging us for the week ahead. But there is more to it than this.

If the body of Christ is to do its job, all the parts, however they are gifted, need to work smoothly together to do their job: living out the gospel of God's restoration work in the world. This appears to be the responsibility of every Christian, whatever their role in the body.

Christ-shaped servanthood has one more characteristic, and it follows from the other two.

3. Servant leaders are a sacrament of the gospel.

There is a distinction between a sign and a sacrament. A sign is arbitrary. For example, a ring can represent marriage, but so could a particular kind of clothing or a specific shape of tattoo. In Maasai culture, husband and wife exchange necklaces. As long as everybody agrees that the thing represents marriage, that's fine.

But a kiss—well, that's different. If you see two people kiss, that is normally a *sign* of love, certainly, but it is more: a kiss is also one experience of the reality of love. There is nothing arbitrary about it, and nothing can replace it. A kiss is a sacrament in a way a ring is not.

In the church, there are many signs of leadership. In the case of ministers, they may wear clerical collars, or special robes, or be called Reverend. There's nothing wrong with those things, of course. We need signs, just as we need signs of marriage. But those signs do not in themselves give anyone a taste of the good news. For some who have been burned by church, those things might even be very bad news.

Christians, as they exercise their giftedness, are more like a kiss than a ring. They are a sacrament of the gospel, not just a sign.

This seems like a huge responsibility, and it is. But startling though it may seem, it is pretty clearly something Jesus taught. Certainly, he never used the word *sacrament*, but listen to this. There are not many sayings that occur in all four of the Gospels, so when they do occur, it's worth paying attention. One of these is phrased like this: "Whoever welcomes you welcomes me," or "Whoever listens to you listens to me."[4] We might assume Jesus is referring only to the apostles—that would let the rest of us off the hook—but on one occasion, he actually uses this saying against the Twelve, which suggests that it is meant for more of us than just the Twelve:[5] "He took a little child and put it among them; and taking it in his arms, he said to them, 'Whoever welcomes one such child in my name welcomes me, and whoever welcomes me welcomes not me but the one who sent me'" (Mark 9:36–37).

It seems that Jesus's followers are not so much a sign of Jesus but a sacrament of Jesus. Some may carry a sign, of course, such as a cross around their neck, but that's relatively easy. Our actions and words are intended to represent his so closely that people's response to the disciples counts as their response to Jesus. To interact with a follower of Jesus is to get a taste of his good news.

We would not be human if we did not find this an overwhelming responsibility. The answer is, first of all, not to get uptight about it. The more uptight we are about representing Jesus, the less likely it is to happen. Of course. The second is to say, OK, Jesus, you said this, so presumably you know how it is even possible, and you can make it happen. And the third is to recognize that God is at work in us to become sacraments of Jesus even when we are not aware of it. It is very common, almost universal, for new Christians to say on reflection, "I just saw something different in my Christian friends, and I wanted it."

And trust me, those Christian friends are normally very surprised to hear it: "What, me? There's nothing special about me. I am embarrassed at how bad a disciple I am." There was a book some years ago called *The Good Enough Parent*.[6] Much of the time, if we are seeking to follow Jesus seriously, we are actually a "good enough witness." A friend who doesn't follow Jesus, but who knows that I do, said to me a little while ago, "You really do walk the talk, don't you?" I'm not sure I even remember what it was I'd done, but I certainly didn't consider it significant. To my friend, however, it was noticeable.

This gives me confidence that "God . . . is at work in [me], enabling [me] both to will and to work for his good pleasure" (Phil 2:13). My job is simply to put one foot in front of the other on the road of discipleship day by day.

LEADERSHIP: THE FEW

Having said that leadership is diffused throughout the body of Christ, I'm now going to do what might appear to go against that. I want to discuss what are traditionally regarded as "leadership" gifts of a particular kind: apostle, prophet, evangelist, pastor, and teacher (Eph 4:11). Sometimes they are known by the acronym APEST. (This only works if you substitute "shepherd" for "pastor," of course, but that makes it easier to remember.)

How do I justify this? Simply on the pragmatic basis that these five have a more upfront role in shaping and directing the overall life of a congregation.[7] So although I am reluctant to give the impression that these are more important than other gifts and thus risk creating a class of "elite leaders" (apart from anything else, I don't want to disempower my friend who heads up the flower arranging team), I do want to treat them separately. After all, at the most basic level, someone has to create the cultural and organizational framework within which other leaders, such as my friend, can do their job.[8] And because their job relates to the shaping of a church's whole life and ethos, they are the ones who are best placed to help create a gospel-shaped culture.

However, I do want to offer some modifications to the five-fold structure, so there will be six categories in all. This is because, in practice, the five are seldom discrete, well-defined categories. There are variations and combinations of gifts that are possible and even needed, for reasons that will become obvious. I will begin with the last of the traditional five and work backward.

1. The Pastor and Teacher

For decades, probably centuries, most churches have assumed that their leaders will be pastors. Indeed, the word *pastor* is often synonymous with "the leader of a congregation." They are usually the ones who are seminary trained, ordained, and salaried. This is what we consider normal in church life. But it was not always so. After all, Ephesians 4:11 lists five gifts, of which pastor (and teacher) comes at the end.

One source of our understanding is the Protestant Reformation in the sixteenth century, which has shaped leadership in many Protestant churches ever since. The leading Reformers believed that the first three gifts in the list—the apostles, prophets, and evangelists—were necessary only in the early years of the church. That period came to an end when the church was well established by the fourth century. After that, all that was necessary to maintain the life and health of the church were . . . pastors and teachers. The Great Commission was no longer binding.[9] One Reformation leader, John Calvin, wrote about Ephesians 4, "Of the offices which Paul enumerates, only the last two [pastor and teacher] are perpetual. For God adorned His Church with apostles, evangelists and prophets, only for a time."[10] The only real issue remaining was whether it was necessary for pastoring and teaching to be combined in the same person.[11] (I have known good pastors who could not teach to save their lives and vice versa—and perhaps you have too.)

But there were other Reformers, sometimes called the Radical Reformation or (the word more often used now) the Anabaptist wing, who saw things differently. The Baptist scholar Stuart Murray Williams says that while for the mainstream Reformers, "Europe was still regarded as essentially Christian, in need of doctrinally sound teaching and effective pastoral care, rather than evangelizing . . . the Anabaptists believed that the Great Commission had not yet been fulfilled in Europe, so evangelism was vital. . . . Through the work of their recognized apostles and evangelists . . . they launched a church planting movement across central Europe."[12]

We will discuss apostles and evangelists shortly, but for the moment, let's just note that the Anabaptists relativized the work of pastor/teachers, not dismissing their significance but pointing out that they are not the only kind of church leadership needed in an unchurched culture.

What kind of world do we inhabit today? The answer is obvious. This is not a Christendom world, where most citizens are simply lapsed believers in need of good pastoring and teaching, if that ever existed. Kathleen Norris comments that her husband, toward the end of his life, "described himself as 'a member of a church that no longer exists.'"[13] In the same way, I have heard pastors say, "I was trained for a church that no longer exists." It's an accurate though poignant observation.

It may seem a harsh question, but it needs to be asked: In a post-Christendom world, where a growing number know nothing of the reality of the Christian faith, do we still need pastors and teachers? My own answer would be yes, we still need them, but perhaps not in the way we thought of them before. Pastors and teachers are not meant, were never meant, to function in isolation as "The Leader of a Congregation." The healthy norm is that they function alongside, and with equal authority to, people who have other gifts—particularly the other leadership gifts.

Of course, it would be possible to tip the balance in the opposite direction and relegate pastor/teachers to a secondary place. But if the ranks of leadership are taken over by other kinds of leaders, who are by definition less pastoral, the church will die. Those with pastoral and teaching gifts come into their own when set in the context of other gifts—apostle, prophet, and evangelist. None will not survive by themselves—they're not meant to—but all will thrive if they see their work as complementary and work together. Almost like the parts of a body. Hmmm, sounds familiar.

2. The Palliative Care Pastor

Here's the first variation on the traditional understanding of the five categories. Many churches will not survive the next ten years—in some cases the next five years, especially following COVID-19. It would be nice to believe otherwise—and of course some can be given new life. It is dangerous to underestimate the grace and power of God. But barring a miracle, many will close their doors. What kind of leadership do they need? I see it as a form of pastoring that provides palliative care for dying congregations.

When I was working on my doctor of ministry some years ago, among my fellow students was a woman who, with her husband, was pastoring a small ethnic Byzantine Catholic congregation, originally from central Europe. The young people were long gone, and the community of those who still spoke their mother tongue was shrinking. Humanly speaking, there was no way that congregation would ever grow. The pastor told me, "My husband and I feel called to minister to this congregation until the last person dies."

I am in awe of people who have that kind of calling, and I am sure I could never fulfil it myself (have I mentioned that leadership is related to giftedness?), but the need for "congregational palliative care" is both crucial and growing. Congregations die all the time—just as (please God) new churches are born all the time—but to help them die with dignity and even joy is crucial. God loves these people, after all. Often, they have served God faithfully for long decades, through thick and thin. There are sad stories of how such churches have been closed with needless clumsiness and lasting hurt.

Might there be such a thing as pastors who have the leadership skills to give palliative care to dying churches? My friend and her husband were certainly that kind of leader. And their ministry is just as much a gospel-focused, Jesus-centered ministry as any other. After all, the gospel has things to say in word and deed to communities at the end of their lives just as much as to individuals in palliative care.

Of course, we would need to be careful if such a role were officially recognized, since it would create—what shall we call them?—delicate situations. We would not want such pastors to be labeled "Rev. Death" and their appointment to be greeted with dread. ("Is it really that bad, pastor? How long have we got?") But such things can be worked out.

3. The Evangelist

A friend has pointed out that Jesus's parable of the lost sheep (Luke 15:4–7) implicitly criticizes leaders who care only about the ninety-nine sheep already safely in the fold and ignore the one that is lost out in the wilderness. Why then, she asks, do our seminaries continue to train pastors who care only for the ninety-nine and who have no interest or ability to help their congregations go after the missing? Were we not listening?[14]

Traditionally, those who search for the one lost sheep are called evangelists.[15] How are they necessary to the formation of a gospel-shaped church? It's obvious, isn't it: they communicate the good news of Jesus to those who don't know it. They pass on information—about God, about Jesus, about God's love for the world, about Jesus's invitation to discipleship—that people would not otherwise have. They may do it in different ways, of course: through personal conversation, or through preaching, or through study groups, or through writing, or in online environments. Whichever it may be, at the heart of it, the work of the evangelist is simply the communication of the gospel.

I know, I know, the popular image of the evangelist is terrible. We have talked about that. But as so often happens, it is the caricature that catches the popular imagination, and the real deal goes under the radar.

Here's an example of that contrast from my own experience. People in and out of the church love to mock TV preachers. I find they make me sad and frustrated rather than amused, but then I suppose in a way I was spoiled. When I began to do evangelistic speaking on university campuses, people asked, "Where did you learn to do it this way?" And in my naivety, I responded, "Um, doesn't everyone do it this way?" The answer, of course, was no. The different model I had encountered and learned from was a British one. (I have been in North America over forty years and outgrew my sense that British is best long ago, so I hope this has a measure of objectivity.) I heard many evangelistic preachers who were clear, witty, widely read, biblical, academically sound (but not arid), respectful, relevant, nonpreachy, nonmanipulative, and challenging. Many were also pastors of local churches, not "professional" evangelists. At the time, I assumed this was normal for evangelists, and I tried to model myself on them.[16]

So there is a "better way" for evangelistic speakers. But the same is true for "conversational evangelists." They are not the people who buttonhole strangers at a bus stop and force conversations about faith on them. They are people who frequently have natural and winsome conversations about Christ and Christian faith without embarrassment and without putting pressure on the other person. They are also good at creating curiosity about Christian faith without really trying. Sometimes, for good reason, these people resist the label "evangelist"—"Good heavens, that's the *last* thing I would want to be called!"—and I for one don't want to force the term on them lest it make them self-conscious and inhibit their ministry. They might even start reading books about evangelism and (God forbid) taking training courses on evangelism—and that would be the end. They are just doing what comes naturally (to them anyway), doing what God has made them to do. Better to let them simply get on with it.

But we do need to pray for more people with gifts in evangelism—whether in public speaking (preferably not in a church building) or simply in one-on-one conversation. If the heart of a healthy church is a grasp of the gospel of Jesus and the work of the pastor/teacher is to help nurture the community in its discipleship, then the task of the evangelist is to explain what is going on to people who are new and don't understand. If the pastor/teacher is the voice to the gathered community, the evangelist is the voice to the world outside. Both are needed.

And the need is urgent. After all, it's no longer a matter of ninety-nine in the fold and one outside. Increasingly, those numbers are reversed.

4. The Prophet

The simplest definition of a prophet is someone who speaks for God. Specifically, it is someone who reminds God's people where they have come from and where God is calling them to go. In other words, someone who recalls the church to the gospel story they are part of. And sometimes it is necessary to do that by pointing out that we have gotten sucked into an alternative story that is not good news. We talked earlier about the church's tendency to become inward looking. The prophet challenges the church to obey the gospel and turn outward again.

Walter Brueggemann suggests that these two aspects can be summarized by the words *criticize* and *energize*.[17] The criticism is backward looking, in the sense of challenging the church, "Look, have you forgotten who God called us to be?" And the energizing is forward looking, in the sense of encouraging the church: "Look what a glorious future God has called us to. Let's abandon this deceptive detour we have got stuck in and start following Jesus afresh."

On a small scale, this is what the three guys who wanted to replace the church hall with a low-rent apartment building (chapter 8) were doing: on the one hand, they were saying, "If we simply rebuild the church hall, we are thinking only of ourselves" (criticizing), and on the other hand they were saying, "Hasn't God called us to love our neighbor? Wouldn't this be a better way to do that?" (energizing). If you worry that this is too trivial an example for a grandiose thing like prophecy, Brueggemann is encouraging: "The issues of God's freedom and his will for justice are not always and need not be expressed primarily in the big issues of the day. They can be discerned wherever people try to live together and worry about their future and their identity."[18]

So how does prophecy help us grow into a gospel-shaped church? This example of the church hall actually helps. The church is the community of disciples of Jesus, called to work under his leadership in the fulfilment of the gospel promise to renew all things. But life being what it is, and culture being what it is, and human nature being what it is, we get off track. We behave as if Christianity is a religion. We treat it as existing just for our comfort. We engage in culture wars and liturgy wars and doctrinal wars among ourselves. We forget what we are all about.

The prophet is the person who says, "Wait a minute. What about the gospel? What about the call of God?" And that leads straight back to the original call of Jesus to "repent and believe," to give up on your own ideas of what life and church are about and get back on track in following him. That's prophecy: the renewed call to Jesus and the mission of his gospel. Without that, we too easily lose the plot and get offtrack.

Having called this a gift, it is worth noting that prophecy, like the other gifts, is on a kind of spectrum. At one end are people whose primary gift is this kind of prophecy. At the other end are what I would call "occasional prophets," like those three guys with bees in their bonnets about low-cost housing. There is or there should be something prophetic, at least sometimes, about a pastor and teacher, not to mention an evangelist. Indeed, any follower of Jesus in some measures "speaks for God" in this way, at least from time to time.

5. The Apostle

For a long time in the twentieth century, there was a debate about whether apostles exist today, or whether *apostle* is a term that should be reserved to refer to "the Twelve" who were sent by Jesus to begin the church. John Stott made a helpful distinction that enabled the conversation to move forward: that we keep the word *apostle* to describe the role of the first disciples and use the adjective *apostolic* to describe the actions of those who pioneer the work of the church today.[19] It's a good way of differentiating.

What do those with apostolic gifts do today? The word *apostle* literally means "sent one." So it seems to me a legitimate application of the word to say one of the primary functions of an apostle is to be sent by an existing Christian community to start new Christian communities where there are no churches.[20] These will normally be places where existing churches can never go—new churches that reflect the culture of their context. Those churches have mission in their DNA from day one and try to be a gospel presence in that place.

Apostolic leaders, like other leaders, normally have a mixture of gifts, of which pioneering is the strongest. They will usually have gifts in evangelism, moving as comfortably in secular culture as in church culture. They will know how to pull innovative teams together, usually have a track record of starting things, and have a competent grasp of orthodox theology. (The last may seem counterintuitive but is particularly important for apostolic leaders because, in the new situation, there is no existing congregation already familiar with the faith.) The apostolic leader will also have something of the pastor in them to care for and guide their new flock—though this can create tension with the apostolic gift![21]

Where do these people come from? Most churches are hardly overflowing with them. In many cases, we will need to recruit these pioneers rather than waiting for them to come to us. Often, they will have shown their ability to start things from scratch already. One of the most creative church planters I know is very gifted in IT and some twenty years ago started a web hosting company that continues to thrive today, long after he left to become a church planter.[22]

Others have a latent pioneering gift that only the trained eye would discern. One leader I know spotted gifts for church planting in his dentist of all unlikely people (as the short-sighted among us might think) and persuaded him to switch vocations.

By the same token, the kind of people who are gifted to pioneer new congregations have not usually considered ordination in a denomination, simply because their image of ministry leadership is the traditional one of pastor and teacher—and they know that it is not for them. (I wouldn't be surprised if the dentist thought that way.) We need to persuade such people that they are exactly who the church needs and train them appropriately.

For many churches, particularly in mainline denominations, the problem is that those who come up through our churches' "farm system" know little apart from life in the traditional congregations they come from and have recognized that they have gifts for . . . traditional ministry. As a result, denominations often do not recognize the very people they need. One gifted evangelist I know was told by his denominational leaders that they would "not be ready for someone like you" for another ten years. The evangelist promptly went off and got himself accredited in a more broad-minded denomination that welcomed his gifts. Frankly, the denomination that refused him may not be around in another ten years—precisely because of that attitude.

6. The Turnaround Leader

Here's another challenge to any attempt to make the fivefold ministry a hard-and-fast list. These days, there is a need for leaders who can help declining congregations change from simply looking after their existing members to understanding that they are called to participate in the mission of God—the sort of scenario considered in chapter 8. Such leaders are required to have a rare and unusual mixture of gifts.

Let's ask first, Why is turnaround ministry difficult? Well, for one reason, the changes required are pretty fundamental. In all likelihood, it will involve changing the congregation's understanding of the gospel, which will in turn require an understanding of church and a corresponding change in the way they have done ministry for many decades. Radical change like that is very threatening, not to mention exhausting.

Twenty years ago, in my naivety, I thought that most struggling congregations would be willing and even excited to make this kind of change in order to thrive again; all they needed was to know how and good leadership to help them do it.

Now I know that is not the case. Given the choice between change and death, many will take time to weigh the options: Change? Death? Hmm . . . and then choose death as the easier choice. Why is it easier? Because all they have to do is keep doing what they have always done. Nothing has to change.

The other reason this has proved difficult is that most pastors, however much they might want to bring about change, simply do not know how. It requires a different skill set. Remember that leadership covers a multitude of gifts, personalities, and abilities. For someone who is primarily a pastor to try to bring about that kind of change in the face of the inevitable resistance is a recipe for conflict, disillusionment, and not uncommonly burnout.

The turnaround leader of a congregation may be called "the pastor" on the church's website, but (not to put too fine a point on it) they may not have the strongest pastoral skills. That's not their greatest strength. Rather, they will normally have a strong combination of the gifts of the evangelist and the prophet: the prophet to remind people (often forcibly) what the gospel is, what a disciple is, and what the church is meant to be[23] and the evangelist both to remind the existing congregation what the good news of Jesus is and also to introduce others to the gospel and to the Jesus who is the heart of the good news.

Of course, there are some congregations that will choose the painful road of change. They need turnaround leaders with clear vision and thick skins and compassion and stick-to-it-iveness—not to mention lots of love—to guide them through the transition. So though the turnaround pastors may need more of the gifts of the prophet and the evangelist, some measure of a pastor's heart will be helpful too.[24]

LEADERSHIP AND THE GOSPEL

These gifts sound very different, and of course they are. But they work together toward a common goal—enabling the church to fulfil its calling. In their distinct ways, they speak, and live, and serve in such a way that the church learns more and more to embrace the good news that Jesus brought of God's determination to renew all things. We can think of it this way:

- *Pastors and teachers* lead God's people to know the gospel in mind and heart and life and help form them as Jesus's apprentices.

- *Evangelists* explain the gospel to people outside the church—although in my experience, they can often be helpful in explaining it to insiders too.

- *Prophets* remind people, often forcefully and directly, of the gospel story, recall them from sin, and encourage them forward.

- And those with *apostolic* gifting take the good news to places where it is not known and spearhead efforts to establish new gospel communities there.

To put it another way, the primary calling of any Christian community is to be disciples of Jesus, learning week by week and day by day to follow him in his world. And God equips the church with a range of gifts, distributed lavishly, to enable us to do that. Our job is to discover, nurture, and exercise as wide a range of those gifts as possible. All are needed. That's why such gifts were given.

CONCLUSION
The Gospel and New Beginnings

For some readers, this book will have covered very familiar ground. For others, it will be new, even disturbing. One friend, a lifelong Anglican, having read the manuscript, commented, "I just think you and I believe in very different churches." He is correct. (Happily, we are still friends!) As he realized, I am offering a model of church that is very different from that which many of us grew up with.

The underlying tension between old and new is not exactly a modern one. It probably began with the invention of the wheel. ("It'll only lead to trouble, you mark my words!") Certainly, in church life, change and tradition sometimes seem like opposites. On the one hand, we hear, "We have our ancient traditions. We love them and we're proud of them. They must not change." But on the other hand, there is also the cry, "The church needs to change with the times. We need to find ways to be relevant."

I've thought about this a lot and finally stumbled upon an insight that I find very freeing: *change is itself part of Christian tradition.* Two Lutheran theologians summarize the paradox very neatly: "To be itself, the gospel speaks to the living hopes and fears of its actual hearers; to be itself, the gospel changes."[1] For the unchanging gospel to do its work, it has to change. And so therefore does the church, because it is nothing if it is not a vehicle for the gospel.

Of course, change is seldom easy. Tolkien describes how this was true for the Elves in *The Lord of the Rings*: "Mere *change* as such is not represented as 'evil': it is the unfolding of the story and to refuse this is of course against the design of God. But the Elvish weakness is in these terms naturally to regret the past, and to become unwilling to face change: as if a man were to hate a very long book still going on, and wished to settle down in a favourite chapter.... They desired some 'power' over things as they are ... to arrest change, and keep things always fresh and fair."[2]

Change is simply "the unfolding of the story," and the story is "the design of God." Stories move forward, or they cease to be stories and become pictures. God's story continues to unfold, and to be a disciple of Jesus is to be committed to God's story and hence to change. We cannot afford to get stuck in our favorite chapter, as churches can do. When people complain that change is upsetting cherished traditions, the answer for the Christian is that change is an integral part of our tradition. Our God is the God who is always doing new things (Isa 43:19)—a new covenant, a new birth, a new commandment, a new name, and ultimately a new heaven and a new earth—until all that is wrong in the world has been put right.

C. S. Lewis suggests that even after the book of Revelation has closed, the newness does not end. In *The Last Battle*, after the children witness the end of Narnia, he writes, "Now at last they were beginning Chapter One of the Great Story, which no one on earth has read: which goes on forever: in which every chapter is better than the one before."[3]

So we return to the theme of this book: the good news of Jesus Christ. Remember the words of Colossians: "[Jesus Christ] was supreme in the beginning and—leading the resurrection parade—he is supreme in the end. From beginning to end he's there, towering far above everything, everyone. So spacious is he, so roomy, that everything of God finds its proper place in him without crowding. Not only that, but all the broken and dislocated pieces of the universe—people and things, animals and atoms—get properly fixed and fit together in vibrant harmonies, all because of his death, his blood that poured down from the cross" (Col 1:15–20 MSG).

And us? We are "a case study of what he does," called to repent of our self-directed lives and give ourselves instead to being apprentices of Jesus—the Jesus through whom all things were made, who lived among us to model a truly human life by living in God's way, who died on the cross for our sins, and who rose again to inaugurate this final phase of God's renewing work.

Are we still nervous? That's natural. Maybe we need a clearer image of this God who calls us to be coworkers. For some of us, one of the most helpful images is that of Aslan the lion, the Christ figure in Lewis's Narnia stories. When the children first arrive in Narnia and hear about Aslan, the son of the great emperor across the sea, at first they assume he is a man. Then they learn that their image is wrong—that he is a lion. But of course, their image of a lion is not quite right either.

Susan asks the beavers, "Is he—quite safe?" and Mr. Beaver replies, in one of the finest theological insights of the last two thousand years, "Safe? Who said anything about safe? Course he isn't safe. But he's good. He's the King, I tell you."[4]

To follow Jesus is to follow one who is not safe—not least because he is always doing new things—but he is good, and all will work out for our good and the creation of a new heaven and a new earth, whatever the challenges along the way. He's the king, I tell you.

ACKNOWLEDGMENTS

A book is never really the work of one person. The person whose name appears on the cover may be called "the author," but every author has been shaped by a community or communities, and I am no exception.

Some of the people in those communities I am aware that I have been shaped by, and many of their names appear in the notes. Usually they are not people I know (or knew) personally, but they are part of my shaping community all the same. Other members of those communities I do indeed know personally. Most of them are not people whose names appear, and may never appear, in a bibliography. That does not mean that their contribution is less valuable. Indeed, in some ways it is more so, because it is directly in response to what I have written. If you like, theirs is not so much a background influence as a foreground influence.

Thus I want to acknowledge a number of wise and discerning friends, some of them new friends, others friends of (very) long standing, who read the whole manuscript and made comments that have reshaped the text in several places. I want to extend particular thanks to Roger Briggs, Mae Cox, Peter Dent, Pilar Gateman, Ross Lockhart, Harold Percy, Chris Schoon, and Mickeelie Webb for their help. It seems appropriate to the theme of this book that among them they represent Anglican, Baptist, Christian Reformed, and Presbyterian churches!

I need to single out Sarah Robinson, my youngest reader—the only millennial—who gave me innumerable meticulous and insightful comments, not to mention fearlessly honest criticisms, more than I could ask or imagine, and made this a better book.

But there is a yet wider community of influencers, and it consists of those who have listened to the contents of this book at various embryonic stages: those at clergy conferences, denominational conferences, and local churches (not least my parish church of St. John the Evangelist, Hamilton) and the many students of Wycliffe College. Their keen listening and insightful questions have helped refine, clarify, and move forward the contents of this book over several years.

Last in terms of chronology, but not least in terms of influence, I want to thank Scott Tunseth, the editor who worked with me on *Evangelism for "Normal" People* back in 2001 and who has now worked with me on this project. Although much water has flowed under many bridges and both of us have become grandfathers since then, our working relationship has remained warm and productive. Once again, I am grateful for his insight, experience, wisdom, and grace.

It goes without saying—but actually should be said—that I could not have done this without the care and support of my closest community of one, Deborah. Thank you. Always. Daily.

For all these, and above all, to the God whose love in Jesus is Good News for the world, I am thankful.

John Bowen
September 2020
Feast of St. Jerome, translator of the Scriptures, 420 CE

NOTES

INTRODUCTION

1   See, for instance, Edith M. Humphrey, *Further Up and Further In: Orthodox Conversations with C. S. Lewis on Scripture and Theology* (New York: St. Vladimir's Seminary, 2017).

2   C. S. Lewis, *Mere Christianity* (1952; repr., San Francisco: Harper-Collins, 2001), viii.

3   An older friend told me that when he was a student, he had invited Lewis to speak to his InterVarsity group in the 1940s. Lewis had (politely) declined, saying that he did not agree with their doctrine of Scripture. Unfortunately, the letter does not survive.

4   *Walking the Good Road: The Gospel and Acts with Ephesians—First Nations Version* (N.p.: Great Thunder, 2017); Fleming Rutledge, *The Crucifixion: Understanding the Death of Jesus Christ* (Grand Rapids: Eerdmans, 2015).

5   I wrote a fuller description of the changes in "Having Second Thoughts about Evangelism," Wycliffe College Institute of Evangelism, October 3, 2014, https://tinyurl.com/yyoq7zcx.

6   C. S. Lewis, "Christianity and Culture," in *Christian Reflections* (1940; repr., Grand Rapids: Eerdmans, 1995), 33.

CHAPTER 1

1   Rodney Stark, *The Rise of Christianity: How the Obscure, Marginal Jesus Movement Became the Dominant Religious Force in the Western World in a Few Centuries* (New York: HarperCollins, 1996), 55–56.

2   It is not clear who first made this statement.

3   In case you care, the total is 116.

4   C. S. Lewis comments, "The gospels . . . are not 'the gospel,' the statement of the Christian belief. They were written for those who had
already been converted, who had already accepted 'the gospel.'"
Lewis, "Modern Translations of the Bible," in J. B. Phillips, *Letters to
Young Churches: A Translation of the New Testament Epistles* (London: Geoffrey Bles, 1947), ix–x.

5   John R. W. Stott, *Basic Christianity* (1958; repr., London: InterVarsity,
1974), 81.

6   The earliest example of this verse being centered out that I am aware
of is in the Anglican Prayer Book of 1662, where it is the first of the
"comfortable [i.e., comforting] words" spoken to those who have con-
fessed their sins. See, for example, Church of England, "The Lord's
Supper or Holy Communion," Book of Common Prayer, accessed
November 14, 2020, https://tinyurl.com/y7tvn2lf.

7   Seventy-two (or two-thirds) of the 116 uses of the word *gospel* are by
him.

8   Christopher Wright draws attention to this text in his book *The Mission of God: Unlocking the Bible's Grand Narrative* (Downers Grove,
IL: InterVarsity, 2006), 63, 328.

9   It's also worth noting that in the evangelistic sermons in Acts, there
is no mention of Christ's atoning death—even in Paul's sermons.
The resurrection was (in some ways, anyway) easier to grasp and to
preach than the atonement.

10   You may recall that this is how C. S. Lewis's *The Lion, the Witch and
the Wardrobe* begins. It was one such child who came to stay with
Lewis during the war who put the idea of a magic wardrobe into his
mind. George Sayer, *Jack: A Life of C. S. Lewis* (Wheaton, IL: Crossway,
1988), 311.

11   Dallas Willard, *Knowing Christ Today: Why We Can Trust Spiritual
Knowledge* (New York: HarperCollins, 2009), Kindle.

12   Anne Snyder, "Wrestling with Loyalty in a Fractured Age," *Comment*,
January 2, 2020, 7.

13   See Matthew Bridges and Godfrey Thring, "Crown Him with Many
Crowns," in *The Hymn Book*, ed. Joint Committee on the Preparation
of a Hymn Book (Toronto: Anglican Church of Canada and the United
Church of Canada, 1971), 373, hymn #367.

14   The word *mission* comes from the same etymological root as "sending," an idea that certainly is present in the New Testament, particularly in the Gospel of John. I discuss this in chapter 4 of *Evangelism
for "Normal" People* (Minneapolis: Augsburg Fortress, 2002). But the
word *mission* turns an action into an abstract concept.

15 Mission should not be confused with missions. Missions are traditionally overseas or in the inner city, "done" by special missionaries,
and supported from "home." Mission is something in the DNA of the
(whole) church, as we shall see.

16 "About every five hundred years the empowered structures of institu-
tionalized Christianity, whatever they may be at that time, become an
intolerable carapace that must be shattered in order that renewal and
new growth may happen." Phyllis Tickle, *The Great Emergence: How
Christianity Is Changing and Why* (Grand Rapids: Baker, 2008), 16.

17 David Bosch credits Hendrik Kraemer as having been the first to recognize this change. Bosch, *Transforming Mission: Paradigm Shifts in
Theology of Mission* (Maryknoll, NY: Orbis, 1993), 7–8.

18 Tim Keller, *The Reason for God: Belief in an Age of Skepticism* (New
York: Dutton, 2008), 223.

19 N. T. Wright, *Thinking in a New Way: How Paul Invented "Christian
Theology,"* e-book from a lecture at Duke Divinity School, Durham, NC,
November 2014, https://ntwrightonline.org/paul-bonus-content.

20 See Bowen, *Evangelism*, 28.

21 Rowan Williams, *Luminaries: Twenty Lives That Illuminate the Christian Way* (London: SPCK, 2019), 50.

22 This approach has been taken by theologians as diverse as Thomas
Aquinas (Roman Catholic) in his *Summa Theologica* (written 1265–
1274), Louis Berkhof (Dutch Reformed) in his *Systematic Theology*
(1932), and more recently, Colin Gunton (English Reformed) in *The
Christian Faith: An Introduction to Christian Doctrine* (Oxford: Blackwell, 2002). John Calvin (Reformed) offers a variation on this approach
by beginning with our knowledge of ourselves and our knowledge of
God in his *Institutes of the Christian Religion* (1559).

23 Most famously, this is the approach of Karl Barth in his *Church Dog-
matics*. It is also the approach of some who might not otherwise
agree with Barth, such as Baptist Bruce Milne's *Know the Truth: A
Handbook of Christian Belief* (London: InterVarsity, 1982).

24 Although his approach is different from mine, John Stott also suggests this starting point in *Evangelical Theology: A Personal Plea
for Unity* (Leicester: InterVarsity, 1999), 29. A somewhat different
approach is taken by Griffith Thomas in a traditional apologia for
Anglicanism, *The Catholic Faith* (1904), which begins with a consideration of personal identity and baptism.

25 I say more about this in chapter 13 of *Evangelism*.

26 Rutledge, *Crucifixion*, 500; italics in original.

27 Horace Bushnell *Vicarious Sacrifice* (1866) in Alister McGrath, *Christian Theology: An Introduction* (Oxford: Blackwell, 1994), 344.

28   The same would be true of the preaching in Acts. The apostles announce the news of Christ and his resurrection and only then call people to repentance.

CHAPTER 2

1   This was the case for the seven commentaries I consulted.

2   Oxford Dictionaries Online, s.v. "repent," accessed November 14, 2020, https://en.oxforddictionaries.com/definition/repent.

3   Oxford Dictionaries Online, s.v. "believe," accessed November 14, 2020, https://en.oxforddictionaries.com/definition/believe_in.

4   Linda Oaks Garrett, "Repentance," in *The Eerdmans Dictionary of the Bible*, ed. David Noel Freedman (Grand Rapids: Eerdmans, 2000), 1118.

5   The First Nations Version of the gospels consistently translates "believe" as "trust." See *Walking the Good Road.*

6   Terrence Prendergast points out that Ezekiel stresses turning from evil, while Jeremiah stresses turning to God. The two are part of the same movement. "Conversion," in *Eerdmans Dictionary*, 277.

7   N. T. Wright, *The Challenge of Jesus: Rediscovering Who Jesus Was and Is* (Downers Grove, IL: InterVarsity, 2015), 44.

8   If we allow for duplicate sayings in the Gospels, it is still around one hundred times. We should also note, however, that Paul never uses the word, although in Acts 9:26, Paul is himself called a disciple.

9   For some fascinating illustrations of the rabbi/disciple relationship, see Michael Griffiths, *The Example of Jesus* (Downers Grove, IL: Inter-Varsity, 1985), 22–25.

10   Thirteen times in the Gospels, Jesus is called "rabbi." Not once does he refuse the title. It is also worth observing that eight of these occurrences are in the Gospel of John. Since John also has the highest Christology among the Gospels, it illustrates the truth that while Jesus is more than a teacher, he is never less than a teacher.

11   I have been deeply influenced in this understanding of discipleship by Robert Brow, *"Go Make Learners": A New Model for Discipleship in the Church* (Wheaton, IL: Harold Shaw, 1981). The book is now available free online at https://tinyurl.com/y5s6uyd5.

12   These four stages have also been labeled unconscious incompetence, conscious incompetence, conscious competence, and unconscious competence. See Martin M. Broadwell, "Teaching for Learning (XVI)," *Gospel Guardian*, February 20, 1969, https://tinyurl.com/y659cy5z.

13   Bosch, *Transforming*, 57.

14 The earliest use of this image of "apprenticeship" I am aware of is from 1945: "Jesus was . . . the master craftsman whom [the disciples] were to follow and imitate. Discipleship was . . . apprenticeship to the work of the kingdom." T. W. Manson, *The Teaching of Jesus* (1945), quoted in Griffiths, *Example*, 48. Dallas Willard uses it frequently in his writings.

15 "[Paul] shows how the gospel creates the church and the church spreads the gospel, and how the gospel shapes the church, as the church seeks to live a life that is worthy of the gospel." Timothy Dudley-Smith, ed., *Authentic Christianity from the Writings of John Stott* (Downers Grove, IL: InterVarsity, 1995), 306.

16 Urban T. Holmes, *Turning to Christ: A Theology of Renewal and Evangelization* (New York: Seabury, 1981), 76.

17 "Jesus intended the sign of baptism to signify the enrolling of learners." Brow, "Go Make," 33.

18 *The Book of Alternative Services of the Anglican Church of Canada* (Toronto: Anglican Book Centre, 1985), 154.

19 See Jana Marguerite Bennett, *Water Is Thicker Than Blood: An Augustinian Theology of Marriage and Singlehood* (New York: Oxford, 2008).

20 Lesslie Newbigin, *The Gospel in a Pluralist Society* (Grand Rapids: Eerdmans/WCC, 1989), 117.

21 This way of understanding baptism is made more complicated by traditions where children in Christian families are dedicated as children and are baptized later, when they make their own profession of faith. In many such cases, the children are living as disciples of Jesus long before they are baptized. The analogy of registering in the school of Jesus doesn't really work in such cases. Maybe a better metaphor would be that discipleship before baptism is like a long engagement that finally culminates in marriage. I am grateful to Mickeelie Webb for drawing my attention to this.

22 Dallas Willard, *The Divine Conspiracy: Rediscovering Our Hidden Life in God* (San Francisco: HarperCollins, 1997), 297–98.

CHAPTER 3

1 "How Long Does It Take to Become a Qualified Plumber?," Answers .com, accessed November 14, 2020, https://tinyurl.com/yysk5jgv.

2 Eugene Peterson used this as the title of his book on discipleship, *A Long Obedience in the Same Direction: Discipleship in an Instant Society* (Downers Grove, IL: InterVarsity, 1980). When he died in 2018,

more than one obituary commented that he had completed his long obedience in the same direction.

3   John P. Bowen, *Growing Up Christian: Why Young People Stay in Church, Leave Church and (Sometimes) Come Back to Church* (Vancouver: Regent College, 2010).

4   H. Carpenter with C. Tolkien, eds., *The Letters of J. R. R. Tolkien* (Boston: Houghton Mifflin, 1981), 82.

5   I wrote about some of these things in the booklet *Tolkien and Faith: The Spiritual Worldview of "The Lord of the Rings"* (Richmond, BC: Digory, 2003). A PDF version may be found here: John Bowen, "Tolkien and Faith: The Spiritual Worldview of *The Lord of the Rings*," Wycliffe College Institute of Evangelism, March 8, 2003, https://tinyurl.com/y6lh6x8u.

6   Bruxy is a Mennonite and not accustomed to having a Communion service every Sunday or feeling the need of it. For other traditions, this is therefore a bit of an overstatement, but a thought-provoking one.

7   Kurt Vonnegut Jr., "Who Am I This Time?," in *Welcome to the Monkey House* (New York: Dell, 1950), 14–26.

8   Alasdair MacIntyre, *After Virtue: A Study in Moral Theory* (Notre Dame, IN: University of Notre Dame Press, 1984), 216.

9   N. T. Wright, *The New Testament and the People of God* (Minneapolis: Fortress, 1992), 140–41 (emphasis in the original).

10   Wright, 141.

11   Bowen, *Evangelism*, chapter 2.

12   J. Richard Middleton and Brian J. Walsh, *Truth Is Stranger Than It Used to Be: Biblical Faith in a Postmodern Age* (Downers Grove, IL: InterVarsity, 1995), 182. One six-act play is Victor Hugo's *Cromwell* (1827).

13   Diana Hartman, "Life's Lie: You Can Be Anything You Want to Be," *Blogcritics*, January 16, 2008. https://tinyurl.com/yylk7ld5.

14   "It is a very silly idea that in reading a book you must never 'skip.' All sensible people skip when they come to a chapter which they find is going to be no use to them." Lewis, *Mere Christianity*, 166.

15   Bruce Trail Conservancy, https://brucetrail.org/.

16   The experiment was described here in 1987: Daniel Goleman, "Long-Married Couples Do Look Alike, Study Finds," *New York Times*, August 11, 1987, https://tinyurl.com/yxfuontv.

17   C. S. Lewis describes the difficulty of praying for Hitler and Stalin: "When you pray for Hitler & Stalin, how do you actually teach yourself to make the prayer real? The two things that help me are (a) A continual grasp of the idea that one is only joining one's feeble little voice

to the perpetual intercession of Christ, who died for those very men (b) A recollection, as firm as one can make it, of all one's own cruelty wh. might have blossomed, under different conditions, into something terrible. You and I are not, at bottom, so different from these ghastly creatures." Lewis, *Letters*, vol. 2 (San Francisco: HarperOne, 2004), 391.

18   Blaise Pascal, *Pensées* (1669; repr., New York: Dutton, 1958), 140.

CHAPTER 4

1   *Book of Alternative Services*. There are six different versions of this prayer, and each has its own distinctive emphasis (pp. 193–210). I have taken the liberty of picking those sections that best illustrate the six-act play.

2   *Book of Alternative Services*, 214–15.

3   Lewis A. Drummond, *Canvas Cathedral: Billy Graham's Ministry through the History of Evangelism* (Nashville: Thomas Nelson 2003), 227. John Stott says something similar: "Conversion must not take the convert out of the world but rather send him [sic] back into it, the same person in the same world, and yet a new person with new convictions and new standards. If Jesus's first command was 'come!' his second was 'go!', that is, we are to go back into the world out of which we have come, and go back as Christ's ambassadors." John R. W. Stott, *Christian Mission in the Modern World* (Downers Grove, IL: InterVarsity, 1975), 121.

4   The story is told in John P. Bowen, ed., *The Missionary Letters of Vincent Donovan 1957–1973* (Eugene, OR: Wipf and Stock, 2011), 214.

5   "I saw many captives crucified, and remembered three of them as my former acquaintance. I was very sorry at this in my mind, and went with tears in my eyes to Titus, and told him of them; so he immediately commanded them to be taken down, and to have the greatest care taken of them, in order to their recovery; yet two of them died under the physician's hands, while the third recovered." Josephus, *The Life of Flavius Josephus* (Radford, VA: Wilder, 2018), Kindle.

6   C. S. Lewis, *The Screwtape Letters: Letters from a Senior to a Junior Devil* (1942; repr., London: Collins Fontana, 1977), 127.

7   Paraphrased in John R. W. Stott, *The Radical Disciple: Some Neglected Aspects of Our Calling* (Downers Grove, IL: InterVarsity, 2009), 37. I have not been able to find the primary source of Temple's words.

8   It will surprise some readers that I have talked about discipleship before discussing the church. How can there be discipleship without the Christian community? And of course, that is correct. At first, I

thought, "Well, chronologically speaking, the foundations of disci-pleship were laid in the Gospels before what we call the church ever came along." More recently, however, I have realized that where Jesus is, there is the church. Could we say that Jesus and the Twelve are an embryonic church—a fresh expression of church, even?

CHAPTER 5

1   Thom Rainer, "13 Issues for Churches in 2013," *ChurchLeaders*, Janu-ary 15, 2013, https://tinyurl.com/y54o8gyu.

2   Peter Brierley, *UK Church Statistics 2: 2010–2020* (Tonbridge, UK: ADBC, 2014). See Evangelical Alliance UK, "How Many Churches Have Opened or Closed," September 18, 2014, https://tinyurl.com/y57hag8p.

3   Brierley's work shows that most of the closures were Anglican, Bap-tist, Methodist, or Presbyterian. Most of the new churches, on the other hand, were Pentecostal, "new churches," or independent or belonged to "smaller denominations."

4   Thom Schultz, "The Church's Frightful Kodak Moment," Holy Soup, January 15, 2014, https://holysoup.com/the-churchs-frightful-kodak-moment/.

5   In the most recent version of the Wikipedia entry, this last phrase is omitted, in spite of (or because of) the fact that in some ways, this is the most significant part. Wikipedia, s.v. "Kodak," last modified Sep-tember 2020, https://en.wikipedia.org/wiki/Kodak.

6   Scott Anthony, "Kodak's Downfall Wasn't about Technology," *Har-vard Business Review*, July 15, 2016, https://hbr.org/2016/07/kodaks-downfall-wasnt-about-technology.

7   Anthony, "Kodak's Downfall."

8   This is a popular summary of the words of business guru Peter Drucker: "Actually 'what is our business' is almost always a difficult question, which can be answered only after hard thinking and study-ing. And the right answer is usually anything but obvious." Drucker, *The Practice of Management* (1959; repr., Dunedin: Allied, 2009), 49.

9   Patten quoted in Bowen, *Missionary Letters*, 215.

10   You can read more about this custom in Vincent Donovan, *Christian-ity Rediscovered* (1978; repr., Maryknoll, NY: Orbis, 2005). Pat Patten went to work in Tanzania as a result of Donovan's influence.

11   Christopher James Schoon, *Cultivating an Evangelistic Charac-ter: Integrating Worship and Discipleship in the Missional Church* (Eugene, OR: Wipf and Stock, 2018), 92.

12   John Calvin, *Institutes of the Christian Religion*, vol. 2, ed. John McNeil, trans. Ford Lewis Battle (Philadelphia: Westminster Press, 1960), 4.1.9.

13   David Bosch notes that "the Belgic Confession (1561) added a third mark of the true church . . . namely the exercise of discipline." Bosch, *Transforming*, 248. Even those churches that still focus on the Word and sacraments have a hard time implementing that one.

14   Bosch, 249. There has been pushback from Lutheran scholars on this claim. It can be modified somewhat, but historian Stephen Neill concludes, "When everything favourable has been said that can be said, and when all possible evidence from the writings of the Reformers have been collected, it all amounts to exceedingly little." Neill, *A History of Christian Missions* (London: Penguin, 1964), 222.

15   This is what C. S. Lewis called "chronological snobbery." Lewis, *Surprised by Joy* (1955; repr., London: HarperCollins, 2002), 240–41.

16   The description of the following four characteristics of church first appeared in Graham Cray, ed., *Mission-Shaped Church: Church Planting and Fresh Expressions of Church in a Changing Context* (London: Church House, 2004), 96–99.

17   The references are (respectively) 1 Corinthians 12:12, 1 Timothy 3:15, 1 Peter 2:5, and Ephesians 6:11.

18   In 1 Corinthians 12:27, Paul says, "You are the body of Christ." In the Greek, he does not say "the body of Christ" because the church at Corinth is not the totality of the body of Christ. But it would be wrong to translate the phrase as "a body of Christ." How can there be many bodies of Christ? English translations avoid the issue by saying "the body of Christ," but Paul's words are more ambiguous, I like to think deliberately.

19   A couple of years after Hurricane Katrina, I visited churches in the devastated parts of New Orleans. Many churches that were part of denominations had been rebuilt and were recovering well. Independent churches in many cases remained abandoned. It was an object lesson in the power of connection.

20   I first met this construct and diagram at the Toronto Vital Church Planting conference in 2008 as part of Lings's two talks. He comments, "At the same 2008 conference, I added that, though the cruciform heart of this diagram was helpful, the four directions view had limitations, suggesting that the further one went in one direction it took one further from the other three, which is not theologically true. I therefore proposed another complementary diagram—a regular tetrahedron—in which all four elements/relationships are of equal significance and are connected to all the other three sides" (personal correspondence). The original and the revised view are

to be found in George Lings, *Reproducing Churches* (Abingdon, UK: Bible Reading Fellowship, 2017), 176–77.

21   Tim Stafford, "Historian Ahead of His Time," *Christianity Today*, February 8, 2007.

22   Andrew Walls, *The Missionary Movement in Christian History: Studies in the Transmission of Faith* (Maryknoll, NY: Orbis, 1996), 3–5.

23   Dana Robert, *Christian Mission: How Christianity Became a World Religion* (Malden, MA: Wiley-Blackwell, 2009), 19–20.

24   Robert, 25.

25   Robert, 23.

26   1 Corinthians 12:12–27.

27   Stephen R. Covey, A. Roger Merrill, and Rebecca R. Merrill, *First Things First* (New York: Simon and Schuster, 1995), 75.

28   Luke 17:32. The story of Lot's wife is told in Genesis 19.

CHAPTER 6

1   I believe this phrase was first used by John Rodgers of Trinity School for Ministry in Pittsburgh at the opening ceremonies of the Wycliffe College Institute of Evangelism in 1991.

2   Mark Molloy, "The Real Story behind a Viral Rembrandt 'Kids on Phones' Photo," *Telegraph*, January 16, 2016, https://tinyurl.com/zp9tgso.

3   This was a slogan of the Canadian Broadcasting Corporation, emphasizing the importance of their radio programs—which by definition have no pictures!

4   James I. Packer, *Fundamentalism and the Word of God* (London: InterVarsity, 1958), 92.

5   Tim Dobbin, "Making Disciples: An Urgent Necessity," in *Good News Church: Celebrating the Legacy of Harold Percy*, ed. John P. Bowen and Michael J. Knowles (Burlington, ON: Castle Quay, 2018).

6   *The Oxford Dictionary of English Etymology* (1966), s.v. "evangelism."

7   I remember, when I was an undergraduate, talking with an old man in a coffee shop once. We started to talk about the gospel, and he immediately said, "Ah, I thought maybe you was a gospeler." It's too bad the word has never caught on.

8   Walter Brueggemann, *Biblical Perspectives on Evangelism: Living in a Three-Storied Universe* (Nashville: Abingdon, 1993), 14.

9   Jack Jackson, "'If Necessary, Use Words': Really?," Wycliffe College Institute of Evangelism, September 28, 2015, accessed November 22, 2016, https://tinyurl.com/y33rlt5x.

10   Ed Stetzer, "Call Yourself a Christian? Start Talking about Jesus Christ," *Washington Post*, May 19, 2016, https://tinyurl.com/y4c8rktk.

11   There are exceptions, of course: someone may come to faith through hearing a Christian radio broadcast, even though they have never had any other Christian connection.

12   See, for example, John Finney, *Finding Faith Today: How Does It Happen?* (Swindon, UK: British and Foreign Bible Society, 1992), 24–25.

13   Anne Lamott, *Traveling Mercies: Some Thoughts on Faith* (New York: Pantheon, 1999), 3.

14   I discuss Jesus's imagery of farming in John 4 and elsewhere, when explaining evangelism as a process, in chapter 6 of *Evangelism*.

15   Alpha is a popular introduction to Christian faith, used for twenty-five years around the world. For more information, see https://alphausa.org or https://alphacanada.org.

16   Sometimes these ways of coming to faith are referred to as "belonging before believing" or "behaving before believing."

17   Robert Bruce was an Anglican missionary in Iran in the late nineteenth century. He wrote, "I am not reaping the harvest; I scarcely claim to be sowing the seed; I am hardly ploughing the soil; but I am gathering out the stones. That too is missionary work, let it be supported by loving sympathy and fervent prayer." Quoted in *Evangelism*, 81.

18   Rebecca Manley Pippert, *Out of the Saltshaker* (Downers Grove, IL: InterVarsity, 1979), 30.

19   C. S. Lewis, "A Slip of the Tongue," in *The Weight of Glory* (New York: Touchstone, 1996), 140–41.

20   Some of these are still online, such as John Bowen, "Trapped in a Free World: The Gospel according to Groundhog Day," Wycliffe College Institute of Evangelism, March 4, 1999, https://tinyurl.com/y5kqacno.

21   John Bowen, "Jesus Is Alive, Elvis Is Alive: What's the Difference?," Wycliffe College Institute of Evangelism, March 8, 1997, https://tinyurl.com/yxvjcdzr.

22   From "The Form of Solemnization of Holy Matrimony," Book of Common Prayer, accessed January 4, 2021, tinyurl.com/1ix7bz7t.

23   2 Corinthians 2:15.

CHAPTER 7

1   The NRSV translates *doulóoh* (to be enslaved) as "become a slave to."

2   I wrote about this in *Evangelism*, chapter 8.

3   There are good reasons for offence and mocking in the gospel (1 Cor 1:23), of course, but these reasons are different. We will come to the more substantial reasons later.

4   Williams, *Luminaries*, 3.

5   Unpublished lecture, Trinity College, Bristol, UK, 1972.

6   Derek Worlock, Roman Catholic archbishop of Liverpool (1976–94), quoted in Michael Paul Gallagher, *Clashing Symbols: An Introduction to Faith and Culture* (Mahwah, NJ: Paulist, 2004), 12.

7   "Before they ate, Faramir and all his men turned west in a moment of silence. Faramir signed to Frodo and Sam that they should do likewise. 'So we always do,' he said as they sat down. . . . 'Have you no such custom?' 'No,' said Frodo, feeling strangely rustic and untutored." J. R. R. Tolkien, *The Lord of the Rings* (London: HarperCollins, 2004), 676.

8   Newbigin, *Gospel*, 195.

9   Mark MacDonald, "Why I Stand with the Five Traditional Leaders of Wet'suwet'en—Especially Now," *Anglican Journal*, February 25, 2020, https://tinyurl.com/y3v6zbpq. MacDonald is the National Indigenous archbishop of the Anglican Church of Canada.

10   The classic exposition of different Christian attitudes toward culture over the centuries is H. Richard Niebuhr's *Christ and Culture* (New York: Harper, 1950). He identifies five main streams. The book has been justly critiqued over the years, but it is still a helpful starting point.

11   See the 1989 York Statement, "Down to Earth: Liturgical Inculturation and the Anglican Communion," in *Inculturation and the Anglican Communion*, ed. David Holeton (Nottingham: Grove, 1990), 8–11.

12   This phrase is attributed to William Temple. See, for example, William Edgar, *Truth in All Its Glory: Commending the Reformed Faith* (Phillipsburg, NJ: P&R, 2004), 2–3.

13   Andy Crouch, *Culture Making: Recovering Our Creative Calling* (Downers Grove, IL: InterVarsity, 2008), 168.

14   Roger Briggs, personal correspondence.

15   J. Richard Middleton, *A New Heaven and a New Earth: Reclaiming Biblical Eschatology* (Grand Rapids: Baker, 2014), 173. Richard Mouw says that the founding fathers of the Reformed tradition "were convinced that the Bible explicitly encourages us to expect an eschatological ingathering of the fruits of humankind's cultural labors." Mouw, *He Shines in All That's Fair* (Grand Rapids: Eerdmans, 2002), 50.

16   *Ethnos* is a Greek word with a wide range of meanings, including "nationality," "race," and "ethnic group."

17   Earl F. Palmer, *Mastering the New Testament: 1, 2, 3 John and Revelation* (Waco, TX: Word, 1982), 246–47.

18   Even so, there are cultural variations as to how the cross is portrayed. The sixteenth-century stone cross of Acolman, outside Mexico City, for example, shows "no blood, no gore, no body even. In place of the Spanish Christ wracked by pain, the cross itself has here become an abstract body of a god, arms outstretched as if in blessing or welcome." Only the face is recognizably human. The missionary friars felt this was more appropriate for "a people so recently inclined to human sacrifice." Bamber Gascoigne, *The Christians* (London: Jonathan Cape, 1977), 182–83.

19   His story is told in Vincent Cronin, *A Pearl to India* (New York: E. P. Dutton, 1959).

20   Neill, *History*, gives two classic examples, one from Pope Gregory I, writing to Augustine of Canterbury in 601 (68–69), and the other from 1659, when the Sacred Congregation for the Propagation of the Faith wrote to its missionaries, asking, "What could be more absurd than to transport France, Spain, Italy or some other European country to China?" (179).

21   I was first alerted to this attitude when reading William H. Willimon's *The Intrusive Word: Preaching to the Unbaptized* (Grand Rapids: Eerdmans, 1994).

22   Walter Brueggemann, *The Prophetic Imagination* (Minneapolis: Fortress, 1978), 11, 13.

23   There is some irony in the fact that the movement to stress the distinctiveness of the church has drawn on the language of secular postmodern literary theory to illustrate its case. Alan Jacobs draws attention to this in his article "A Tale of Two Stanleys," *First Things* 44 (June/July 1994), https://tinyurl.com/yys8dbrw.

24   David Bosch says that Barth "became one of the first theologians to articulate mission as an activity of God himself." Bosch, *Transforming*, 389.

25   The word *confessing* is used here in the sense of "confessing publicly what we believe and stand for."

26   A good summary of the story of the Confessing Church can be found here: Leonore Siegele-Wenschkewitz, "Christians against Nazis: The German Confessing Church," *Christianity Today*, accessed December 4, 2020, https://tinyurl.com/y5ubwxnj.

27   C. S. Lewis disagrees: "I read in a periodical the other day that the fundamental thing is how we think of God. By God Himself, it is not!" Lewis, "The Weight of Glory," in *Screwtape Proposes a Toast* (London: Fontana,

1965), 103. For once I think he is wrong. After all, even if we think God's view of us is an objective reality (which I do), that is still a conviction—one of the most important convictions—we hold in our minds.

28   "Salvation begins with what is usually termed (and very properly) preventing [i.e., prevenient] grace; including the first wish to please God, the first dawn of light concerning his will, and the first slight transient conviction of having sinned against him." John Wesley, *On Working Out Our Own Salvation*, quoted in John R. Tyson, *The Way of the Wesleys: A Short Introduction* (Grand Rapids: Eerdmans, 2014), 57.

29   The doctrine is summarized by Jesus in the Sermon on the Mount: God "makes his sun rise on the evil and on the good, and sends rain on the righteous and on the unrighteous" (Matt 5:45).

30   Richard Mouw recounts the debate about "the antithesis" (between common and special grace) in the Reformed tradition in his book *He Shines in All That's Fair*. Personally, I suspect that the two are not as far apart as the terminology suggests. As Mouw himself says, "For all I know—for all any of us can know—much of what we now think of as common grace may in the end time be revealed to be saving grace" (100).

31   Mouw, 80.

32   "It was the problem of political theology of the German Christians, who believe instead of the Old Testament, in blood and soil of the German Race, and the Germanic historic figure of the victorious Christ, etcetera, etcetera. So to fight against the German Christians, he said there must be no Natural Theology." Jurgen Moltmann, "Jürgen Moltmann on Unfinished Summas and Natural Theology," interview with Tony Jones, PostBarthian, December 2, 2013. https://tinyurl.com/yxb9w72r.

33   Mouw, *He Shines*, 25.

34   Paul Scherer goes as far as to say evangelists should not start "where people are at" because they are "in the wrong place." Scherer, *The Word God Sent* (New York: Harper and Row, 1965), 95, cited in Charles Campbell, *Preaching Jesus: The New Directions for Homiletics in Hans Frei's Postliberal Theology* (Eugene, OR: Wipf and Stock, 2006), 162. Prevenient grace would suggest that nobody is in the wrong place to encounter God's Spirit.

35   A good introduction to Barth's notion of "secular parables" can be found in George Hunsinger's *How to Read Karl Barth: The Shape of His Theology* (Oxford: Oxford University Press, 1993). Hunsinger writes, for example, "Despite appearances, the Word itself is at work in the world incognito, not leaving it destitute but raising up 'witnesses to

the truth from the darkness of the nations' outside the community's own sphere. . . . These secular parables will therefore demand a real hearing from the community, not deflecting it from 'its own mission to preach the one Word of God,' but assisting, comforting, and strengthening it on the way" (255).

36   Anselm, *Cur Deus Homo*, chapter 21, Jasper Hopkins homepage, accessed November 14, 2020, http://jasper-hopkins.info/CurDeusI.pdf.

37   Luther's Latin phrase is *homo incurvatus in se.*

38   George Sumner, former principal of Wycliffe College, Toronto, now Episcopal Bishop of Dallas. Inaugural lecture, "October 6th in Sheraton Hall—an Evening of Celebration," *Insight* magazine, December 1999, 10–11.

CHAPTER 8

1   At least thirty-five states have a Springfield—none of them home to the Simpsons—so I thought this was a safely generic name.

2   Newbigin, *Gospel*, 227.

3   Rowan Williams, "The 'Strength' of the Church Is Never Anything Other Than the Strength of the Presence of the Risen Jesus," *Journal of Fresh Expressions*, Autumn/Winter 2008/9, 13.

4   *American Congregations at the Beginning of the 21st Century: National Congregations Study*, 2019, https://tinyurl.com/yewgs2j. The average is much higher—184—because more than half of all churchgoers attend large churches.

5   *American Congregations*, 9.

6   If the King James Version had stuck with Tyndale's translation of the Greek *ecclesia* as "congregation," not "church," might things be different? We will never know—but I like to think they might. Rowan Williams comments that in the King James Version, "we see a very consistent rearguard action to make Tyndale's English a little bit more restrained." Williams, *Luminaries*, 53.

7   Cam Harder asks the question, If churches lost their buildings, their bank accounts, and their clergy overnight, what would the church be then? Harder, "New Shoots from Old Roots: The Challenge and Potential of Mission in Rural Canada," in *Green Shoots out of Dry Ground*, ed. John P. Bowen (Portland, OR: Wipf and Stock, 2013), 49–62. The answers are, perhaps surprisingly, encouraging.

8   It is worth noting that Jesus equates "for my sake" and "for the sake of the gospel." Jesus is the content of the gospel. The gospel is good news about Jesus.

9   Patty Winsa, "Sale of Local Church Brings a Chance for Reinvention," *Toronto Star*, December 5, 2010, https://tinyurl.com/y6ftrn8c.

10   Philip Jenkins, *The Lost History of Christianity: The Thousand-Year Golden Age of the Church in the Middle East, Africa, and Asia—and How It Died* (San Francisco: HarperOne, 2008).

11   Judy Paulsen, "Being Intentional in Leadership," in Bowen and Knowles, *Good News Church*, 56.

12   John V. Taylor, *The Go-Between God: The Holy Spirit and the Christian Mission* (London: SCM, 1972), 55. Versions of this saying have been variously attributed, but this is the earliest I have come across.

13   This phrase originated with the Fresh Expressions movement in the UK.

14   Personal letter.

15   The pastor tells me she never did discover what happened to the other $20.

16   Joe Friesen, "Attendance Increasing at Theologically Conservative Churches," *Globe and Mail*, November 19, 2016, https://tinyurl.com/y68bjtsj.

17   I have written more fully about this in the booklet *From Visitor to Disciple: Eight Ways Your Church Can Help* (Richmond, BC: Digory, 2005), https://tinyurl.com/y6hmohfj.

18   See, for instance, John Bowen and Harold Percy, *Just the Basics: Teaching the Faith to Beginners* (Richmond, BC: Digory, 2004), https://tinyurl.com/y38rx6pj.

19   Chapter 7, page 113.

20   See Messy Church USA, https://messychurchusa.org; Messy Church Canada, https://messychurch.ca/; and Messy Church UK, https://www.messychurch.org.uk/.

CHAPTER 9

1   Tim Stafford, "Go and Plant Churches of All Peoples: Crusades and Personal Witnessing Are No Longer the Cutting Edge of Evangelism," *Christianity Today*, September 27, 2007, https://tinyurl.com/34vfrh.

2   One of the first attempts to categorize different forms of church planting identified twelve distinct kinds. Cray, *Mission-Shaped Church*, 44.

3   Reginald Stackhouse, "Church Planting in the 1950s: A Historical Perspective," in Bowen, *Green Shoots*, 35–41.

4   For instance, the Pew Research Center reported in 2016, "While nationwide surveys in the 1970s and '80s found that fewer than

one-in-ten U.S. adults said they had no religious affiliation, fully 23% now describe themselves as atheists, agnostics or 'nothing in particular.'" Alan Cooperman and Gregory A. Smith, "The Factors Driving the Growth of Religious 'Nones' in the U.S.," Pew Research Center, September 14, 2016, https://tinyurl.com/y6beq2ja.

5   John P. Bowen, *Churches Turning Outwards: Missional Projects in the Diocese of Toronto, 2017* (Toronto: Anglican Diocese of Toronto, 2017), 33.

6   Bishop Jenny Andison, public lecture, 2017 ReChurch Conference, St. Catharines, Ontario, November 4, 2017.

7   George Lings, *Encountering "The Day of Small Things"* (Sheffield, UK: Church Army, 2017), 18.

8   Lesslie Newbigin, "What Is 'a Local Church Truly United?'" (1976), in *The Ecumenical Movement: An Anthology of Key Texts and Voices*, ed. Michael Kinnamon and Brian E. Cope (Grand Rapids: Eerdmans, 1996), 118.

9   See, for instance, the Presbyterian Church's "1001 Worshipping Communities" project: https://tinyurl.com/y4rxdhvs. The website says it is "using new and varied forms of church for our diverse and changing culture."

10 Newbigin, "What Is a Local Church?," 118.

11 Newbigin, 118.

12 Unpublished lecture, the Vital Church Planting conference, St Paul's Bloor Street, Toronto, May 2011. Quoted with permission.

13 The story of this bookstore, The Dusty Cover, is part of the bigger narrative of the Little Flowers community in Winnipeg, Manitoba, as told in Jamie Arpin-Ricci's *The Cost of Community: Jesus, St. Francis and Life in the Kingdom* (Downers Grove, IL: InterVarsity, 2011).

14 Newbigin, "What Is 'a Local Church'?," 118.

15 John P. Bowen, "Redeeming the Idols," in *Confronting the Idols of Our Age*, ed. Thomas Power (Eugene, OR: Wipf and Stock, 2017), 1–7.

16 The phrase "Small is beautiful" was popularized by E. F. Schumacher's book *Small Is Beautiful: Economics as If People Mattered* (London: Blond and Briggs, 1973).

17 One popular church offered "purge Sundays" a couple of times a year to encourage "Christian tourists" to get involved or to find another church. See Patricia Paddey, "Church Uses 'Purge Sundays' to Send Non-committed Elsewhere," Christianity.ca, accessed November 14, 2020, https://tinyurl.com/yxa4skag.

18 Paul Sparks, Tim Soerens, and Dwight J. Friesen, *The New Parish: How Neighborhood Churches Are Transforming Mission, Discipleship*

and Community (Downers Grove, IL: InterVarsity, 2014). A friend of mine wrote a related book with the wonderful title *No Home like Place*. Leonard Hjalmarson, *No Home like Place: A Christian Theology of Place* (Portland, OR: Urban Loft, 2014).

CHAPTER 10

1   Seventh out of eight gifts listed in Romans 12 and in 1 Corinthians 12.

2   See Romans 12:6–8, 1 Corinthians 12:8–10 and 28, Ephesians 4:11, and 1 Peter 4:9–11.

3   Michael Green, *I Believe in the Holy Spirit* (London: Hodder and Stoughton, 1975), 244.

4   In Matthew and Luke, the saying is connected with the sending out of the Twelve and the seventy, respectively (Matt 10:40 and Luke 10:16). In Mark and Luke, it is Jesus's response to the disciples' bickering over which of them is the greatest (Luke 9:46–48 and Mark 9:37). And in John, it is part of the Upper Room Discourse (John 13:20).

5   In any case, in Luke 10:16 the words are addressed to the seventy, not just the Twelve.

6   Andrew Wake, *The Good Enough Parent: How to Provide for Your Child's Social and Emotional Development* (Bayswater, Victoria, Australia: Palmer Higgs, 2012).

7   Anabaptist scholar John Howard Yoder is passionately "against trying to establish a hierarchy of values among the varied gifts." Yet even he admits, "It could be argued on good sociological grounds that the moderating-presiding function of the elders-pastors is the most significant for the church's capacity to function and survive as a social organism." Yoder, *The Fullness of Christ: Paul's Vision of Universal Ministry* (Elgin, IL: Brethren, 1987), 10.

8   It would take us too far afield to discuss ordination. However, to take the fivefold giftings seriously would require a rethinking of whom we ordain and to what ministry. In particular, the structure of ordination to deacon and then priest (not a word ever used in the New Testament for church leadership) does not allow for the variety of ministry we need. Ordination is usually to the traditional Reformation roles of "word and sacrament," pastor and teacher. This means there is little if any room for recognizing and authorizing other leadership gifts, especially if you regard that structure as a "supernatural order" (R. R. Reno, "Catholicism after 2018," *First Things*, October 2018, https://tinyurl.com/ybptjz8t). If all you have is a hammer, everything

looks like a nail. The Church of England is trying to stretch the traditional structure with its recent creation of "Ordained Pioneer Ministries."

9   Bosch, *Transforming*, 246.

10   John Calvin, *Calvin's New Testament Commentaries: Galatians, Ephesians, Philippians and Colossians* (Grand Rapids: Eerdmans, 1965), 179–80. He does make one exception: "Where religion has broken down, [God] raises up evangelists apart from the church order, to restore the pure doctrine to its firmer position." It would be interesting to know whether he would consider the present day one of those times.

11   Stuart Murray, *Church Planting: Laying Foundations* (Milton Keynes: Paternoster Press, 1998), 97–98. (He added the name Williams later.)

12   Murray, 97–98. In comparison, for the Anabaptists, "Europe was once again a mission field. As at the time of the apostles, the Christian faith had to be introduced anew into a pagan environment." Bosch, *Transforming*, 247.

13   Kathleen Norris, *Acedia and Me: A Marriage, Monks, and a Writer's Life* (New York: Riverhead, 2008), 238.

14   Judy Paulsen, private communication. She points out that in Canada, at least, the proportion is no longer ninety-nine to one but twenty-one to seventy-nine, making this an even more urgent issue. Jesus was concerned for the one; how much more so for the seventy-nine! See "A Spectrum of Spirituality: Canadians Keep the Faith to Varying Degrees, but Few Reject It Entirely," Angus Reid Institute, accessed November 14, 2020, http://angusreid.org/religion-in-canada-150.

15   It is true that Jesus speaks as if this work is the role of the pastor/shepherd, but this is a parable, not a formal discussion of the proper division of labor among church leaders.

16   They included David Watson, David McInnes, Michael Green, John Stott, John Freeth, and Roger Forster. A lot of them were also ordained Anglican clergy. All privileged white European males, I know, but this was the 1970s.

17   Brueggemann, *Prophetic Imagination*, 13.

18   Brueggemann, 110.

19   "To be sure, there are missionaries and church leaders of different kinds who may be described as having an 'apostolic' ministry, but there are no apostles like the Twelve and Paul who were eyewitnesses of the risen Lord." Dudley-Smith, *Authentic Christianity*, 284.

20   Apostles are "divinely commissioned missionaries and planters of churches." Andrew T. Lincoln, *Word Bible Commentary*, vol. 42,

Ephesians (Nashville: Word, 1990), 249. "It is certainly possible to argue that there are people with apostolic ministries of a different kind, including episcopal jurisdiction, pioneer missionary work, church planting, itinerant leadership, etc." John R. W. Stott, *God's New Society: The Message of Ephesians* (Downers Grove, IL: Inter-Varsity, 1979), 161.

21 "For [Vincent Donovan], a missionary is not a permanent pastor absorbed in serving existing Christian communities. We, his friends, nevertheless teased him, because we were witnesses to his persistent pastoral empathy and compassion. He would graciously modify his best laid plans to keep free of pastoral entanglements whenever people presented themselves to him with needs that in Masailand [sic] were invariably genuine and serious." Eugene Hillman, "Vincent Donovan as Friend and Missiologist," in Donovan, *Christianity Rediscovered*, 162.

22 StormWeb, http://www.stormweb.ca.

23 John Stott said once that if he were going to a new church, he would spend the first year teaching the doctrine of the church. I have been unable to trace the source of this quotation.

24 Lessons from one such pastor are documented in Bowen and Knowles, *Good News Church*.

CONCLUSION

1 Eric Gritsch and Robert W. Jenson, *Lutheranism: The Theological Movement and Its Confessional Writings* (Philadelphia: Fortress, 1983), 3.

2 Carpenter with Tolkien, *Letters*, 236.

3 C. S. Lewis, *The Last Battle* (1956; repr., London: Fontana, 1980), 173.

4 C. S. Lewis, *The Lion, the Witch and the Wardrobe* (1950; repr., London: Lions, 1980), 75.

BIBLIOGRAPHY

American Congregations at the Beginning of the 21st Century: National Congregations Study. 2019. https://tinyurl.com/yewgs2j.

Angus Reid Institute. "A Spectrum of Spirituality: Canadians Keep the Faith to Varying Degrees, but Few Reject It Entirely." Accessed November 14, 2020. http://angusreid.org/religion-in-canada-150.

Anthony, Scott. "Kodak's Downfall Wasn't about Technology." *Harvard Business Review*, July 15, 2016. https://tinyurl.com/hzm9cjz.

Arpin-Ricci, Jamie. *The Cost of Community: Jesus, St. Francis and Life in the Kingdom.* Downers Grove, IL: InterVarsity, 2011.

Bennett, Jana Marguerite. *Water Is Thicker Than Blood: An Augustinian Theology of Marriage and Singlehood.* New York: Oxford, 2008.

The Book of Alternative Services of the Anglican Church of Canada. Toronto: Anglican Book Centre, 1985.

Bosch, David. *Transforming Mission: Paradigm Shifts in Theology of Mission.* Maryknoll, NY: Orbis, 1991.

Bowen, John, and Harold Percy. *Just the Basics: Teaching the Faith to Beginners.* Richmond, BC: Digory, 2004. https://tinyurl.com/y38rx6pj.

Bowen, John P. *Churches Turning Outwards: Missional Projects in the Diocese of Toronto, 2017.* Toronto: Anglican Diocese of Toronto, 2017.

———. *Evangelism for "Normal" People.* Minneapolis: Augsburg Fortress, 2002.

———. *From Visitor to Disciple: Eight Ways Your Church Can Help.* Richmond, BC: Digory, 2005. https://tinyurl.com/y6hmohfj.

———. *Growing Up Christian: Why Young People Stay in Church, Leave Church and (Sometimes) Come Back to Church.* Vancouver: Regent College, 2010.

———. "Having Second Thoughts about Evangelism." Wycliffe College Institute of Evangelism, October 3, 2014. https://tinyurl.com/yyoq7zcx.

———. "Jesus Is Alive, Elvis Is Alive: What's the Difference?" Wycliffe College Institute of Evangelism, March 8, 1997. https://tinyurl.com/yxvjcdzr.

——, ed. *The Missionary Letters of Vincent Donovan 1957–1973*. Eugene, OR: Wipf and Stock, 2011.

——. "Redeeming the Idols." In *Confronting the Idols of Our Age*, edited by Thomas Power, 1–7. Eugene, OR: Wipf and Stock, 2017.

——. *Tolkien and Faith: The Spiritual Worldview of "The Lord of the Rings."* Richmond, BC: Digory, 2003. https://tinyurl.com/y6lh6x8u.

——. "Trapped in a Free World: The Gospel according to Groundhog Day." Wycliffe College Institute of Evangelism, March 4, 1999. https://tinyurl.com/y5kqacno.

Bridges, Matthew, and Godfrey Thring. "Crown Him with Many Crowns." In *The Hymn Book*, edited by the Joint Committee on the Preparation of a Hymn Book. Toronto: Anglican Church of Canada and the United Church of Canada, 1971.

Brierley, Peter. *UK Church Statistics 2: 2010–2020*. Tonbridge, UK: ADBC, 2014. https://tinyurl.com/y57hag8p.

Broadwell, Martin M. "Teaching for Learning (XVI)." *Gospel Guardian*, February 20, 1969. https://tinyurl.com/y659cy5z.

Brow, Robert. *"Go Make Learners": A New Model for Discipleship in the Church*. Wheaton, IL: Harold Shaw, 1981. https://tinyurl.com/y5s6uyd5.

Brueggemann, Walter. *Biblical Perspectives on Evangelism: Living in a Three-Storied Universe*. Nashville: Abingdon, 1993.

——. *The Prophetic Imagination*. Minneapolis: Fortress, 1978.

Calvin, John. *Calvin's New Testament Commentaries: Galatians, Ephesians, Philippians and Colossians*. Grand Rapids: Eerdmans, 1965.

——. *Institutes of the Christian Religion*. Vol. 2, edited by John McNeil, translated by Ford Lewis Battle. Philadelphia: Westminster Press, 1960.

Campbell, Charles. *Preaching Jesus: The New Directions for Homiletics in Hans Frei's Postliberal Theology*. Eugene, OR: Wipf and Stock, 2006.

Carpenter, H., with C. Tolkien, eds. *The Letters of J. R. R. Tolkien*. Boston: Houghton Mifflin, 1981.

Church of England. *Worship Texts and Resources*. https://tinyurl.com/y7tvn2lf.

Cooperman, Alan, and Gregory A. Smith. "The Factors Driving the Growth of Religious 'Nones' in the U.S." Pew Research Center, September 14, 2016. https://tinyurl.com/y6beq2ja.

Covey, Stephen R., A. Roger Merrill, and Rebecca R. Merrill. *First Things First*. New York: Simon and Schuster, 1995.

Cray, Graham, ed. *Mission-Shaped Church: Church Planting and Fresh Expressions of Church in a Changing Context*. London: Church House, 2004.

Cronin, Vincent. *A Pearl to India*. New York: E. P. Dutton, 1959.

Crouch, Andy. *Culture Making: Recovering Our Creative Calling.* Downers Grove, IL: InterVarsity, 2008.

Dobbin, Tim. "Making Disciples: An Urgent Necessity." In *Good News Church: Celebrating the Legacy of Harold Percy,* edited by John P. Bowen and Michael J. Knowles, 103–116. Burlington, ON: Castle Quay, 2018.

Donovan, Vincent. *Christianity Rediscovered.* 1978. Reprint, Maryknoll, NY: Orbis, 2005.

Drucker, Peter. *The Practice of Management.* 1959. Reprint, Dunedin: Allied, 2009.

Drummond, Lewis A. *Canvas Cathedral: Billy Graham's Ministry through the History of Evangelism.* Nashville: Thomas Nelson 2003.

Dudley-Smith, Timothy, ed. *Authentic Christianity from the Writings of John Stott.* Downers Grove, IL: InterVarsity, 1995.

Edgar, William. *Truth in All Its Glory: Commending the Reformed Faith.* Phillipsburg, NJ: P&R, 2004.

Evangelical Alliance UK. "How Many Churches Have Opened or Closed." September 18, 2014. https://tinyurl.com/y57hag8p.

Finney, John. *Finding Faith Today: How Does It Happen?* Swindon, UK: British and Foreign Bible Society, 1992.

Friesen, Joe. "Attendance Increasing at Theologically Conservative Churches." *Globe and Mail,* November 19, 2016. https://tinyurl.com/y5cmh9k3.

Freedman, David Noel, ed. *The Eerdmans Dictionary of the Bible.* Grand Rapids: Eerdmans, 2000.

Gallagher, Michael Paul. *Clashing Symbols: An Introduction to Faith and Culture.* Mahwah, NJ: Paulist, 2004.

Gascoigne, Bamber. *The Christians.* London: Jonathan Cape, 1977.

Goleman, Daniel. "Long-Married Couples Do Look Alike, Study Finds." *New York Times,* August 11, 1987. https://tinyurl.com/yxfuontv.

Green, Michael. *I Believe in the Holy Spirit.* London: Hodder and Stoughton, 1975.

Griffiths, Michael. *The Example of Jesus.* Downers Grove, IL: InterVarsity, 1985.

Gritsch, Eric, and Robert W. Jenson. *Lutheranism: The Theological Movement and Its Confessional Writings.* Philadelphia: Fortress, 1983.

Gunton, Colin. *The Christian Faith: An Introduction to Christian Doctrine.* Oxford: Blackwell, 2002.

Harder, Cam. "New Shoots from Old Roots: The Challenge and Potential of Mission in Rural Canada." In *Green Shoots out of Dry Ground,* edited by John P. Bowen, 49–62. Portland, OR: Wipf and Stock, 2013.

Hartman, Diana. "Life's Lie: You Can Be Anything You Want to Be." *Blogcritics*, January 16, 2008. https://tinyurl.com/yylk7ld5.

Hillman, Eugene. "Vincent Donovan as Friend and Missiologist." In *Christianity Rediscovered*, by Vincent Donovan, 160–165. Maryknoll, NY: Orbis, 2005.

Hjalmarson, Leonard. *No Home like Place: A Christian Theology of Place.* Portland, OR: Urban Loft, 2014.

Holeton, David, ed. *Inculturation and the Anglican Communion.* Nottingham: Grove, 1990.

Holmes, Urban T. *Turning to Christ: A Theology of Renewal and Evangelization.* New York: Seabury, 1981.

Humphrey, Edith M. *Further Up and Further In: Orthodox Conversations with C. S. Lewis on Scripture and Theology.* New York: St. Vladimir's Seminary, 2017.

Hunsinger, George. *How to Read Karl Barth: The Shape of His Theology.* Oxford: Oxford University Press, 1993.

Jackson, Jack. "'If Necessary, Use Words': Really?" Wycliffe College Institute of Evangelism, September 28, 2015. https://tinyurl.com/y33rlt5x.

Jacobs, Alan. "A Tale of Two Stanleys." *First Things* 44 (June/July 1994). https://tinyurl.com/yys8dbrw.

Jenkins, Philip. *The Lost History of Christianity: The Thousand-Year Golden Age of the Church in the Middle East, Africa, and Asia—and How It Died.* San Francisco: HarperOne, 2008.

Josephus. *The Life of Flavius Josephus.* Radford, VA: Wilder, 2018. Kindle.

Keller, Tim. *The Reason for God: Belief in an Age of Skepticism.* New York: Dutton, 2008.

Lamott, Anne. *Traveling Mercies: Some Thoughts on Faith.* New York: Pantheon, 1999.

Lewis, C. S. "Christianity and Culture." In *Christian Reflections*, 12–36. 1940. Reprint, Grand Rapids: Eerdmans, 1995.

———. *The Last Battle.* 1956. Reprint, London: Fontana, 1980.

———. *Letters.* Vol. 2. San Francisco: HarperOne, 2004.

———. *The Lion, the Witch and the Wardrobe.* 1950. Reprint, London: Lions, 1980.

———. *Mere Christianity.* 1952. Reprint, San Francisco: HarperCollins, 2001.

———. "Modern Translations of the Bible." In *Letters to Young Churches: A Translation of the New Testament Epistles*, by J. B. Phillips, vii–x. London: Geoffrey Bles, 1947.

———. *The Screwtape Letters: Letters from a Senior to a Junior Devil.* 1942. Reprint, London: Collins Fontana, 1977.

———. "A Slip of the Tongue." In *The Weight of Glory*, 184–192. New York: Touchstone, 1996.

——. *Surprised by Joy*. 1955. Reprint, London: HarperCollins, 2002.

——. "The Weight of Glory." In *Screwtape Proposes a Toast*, 94–110. London: Fontana, 1965.

Lincoln, Andrew T. *Word Bible Commentary*. Vol. 42, *Ephesians*. Nashville: Word, 1990.

Lings, George. *Encountering "The Day of Small Things."* Sheffield, UK: Church Army, 2017.

——. *Reproducing Churches*. Abingdon, UK: Bible Reading Fellowship, 2017.

MacDonald, Mark. "Why I Stand with the Five Traditional Leaders of Wet'suwet'en—Especially Now." *Anglican Journal*, February 25, 2020. https://tinyurl.com/y3v6zbpq.

MacIntyre, Alasdair. *After Virtue: A Study in Moral Theory*. Notre Dame, IN: University of Notre Dame Press, 1984.

McGrath, Alister. *Christian Theology: An Introduction*. Oxford: Blackwell, 1994.

Middleton, J. Richard. *A New Heaven and a New Earth: Reclaiming Biblical Eschatology*. Grand Rapids: Baker, 2014.

Middleton, J. Richard, and Brian J. Walsh. *Truth Is Stranger Than It Used to Be: Biblical Faith in a Postmodern Age*. Downers Grove, IL: InterVarsity, 1995.

Milne, Bruce. *Know the Truth: A Handbook of Christian Belief*. London: InterVarsity, 1982.

Molloy, Mark. "The Real Story behind a Viral Rembrandt 'Kids on Phones' Photo." *Telegraph*, January 16, 2016. https://tinyurl.com/zp9tgso.

Moltmann, Jurgen. "Jürgen Moltmann on Unfinished Summas and Natural Theology." Interview by Tony Jones. PostBarthian, December 2, 2013. https://tinyurl.com/yxb9w72r.

Mouw, Richard. *He Shines in All That's Fair*. Grand Rapids: Eerdmans, 2002.

Murray, Stuart. *Church Planting: Laying Foundations*. Milton Keynes: Paternoster Press, 1998.

Neill, Stephen. *A History of Christian Missions*. London: Penguin, 1964.

Newbigin, Lesslie. *The Gospel in a Pluralist Society*. Grand Rapids: Eerdmans/WCC, 1989.

——. "What Is 'a Local Church Truly United?'" In *The Ecumenical Movement: An Anthology of Key Texts and Voices*, edited by Michael Kinnamon and Brian E. Cope, 114–121. Grand Rapids: Eerdmans, 1996.

Niebuhr, H. Richard. *Christ and Culture*. New York: Harper, 1950.

Norris, Kathleen *Acedia and Me: A Marriage, Monks, and a Writer's Life*. New York: Riverhead, 2008.

Packer, James I. *Fundamentalism and the Word of God*. London: Inter-Varsity, 1958.

Paddey, Patricia. "Church Uses 'Purge Sundays' to Send Non-committed Elsewhere." Christianity.ca. Accessed November 14, 2020. https://tinyurl.com/yxa4skag.

Palmer, Earl F. *Mastering the New Testament: 1, 2, 3 John and Revelation.* Waco, TX: Word, 1982.

Pascal, Blaise. *Pensées.* 1669. Reprint, New York: Dutton, 1958.

Paulsen, Judy. "Being Intentional in Leadership." In *Good News Church: Celebrating the Legacy of Harold Percy*, edited by John P. Bowen and Michael J. Knowles, 49–62. Burlington, ON: Castle Quay, 2018.

Peterson, Eugene. *A Long Obedience in the Same Direction: Discipleship in an Instant Society.* Downers Grove, IL: InterVarsity, 1980.

Pippert, Rebecca Manley. *Out of the Saltshaker.* Downers Grove, IL: Inter-Varsity, 1979.

Prendergast, Terrence. "Conversion." In *Eerdmans Dictionary of the Bible*, edited by David Noel Freedman, 277. Grand Rapids: Eerdmans, 2000.

Rainer, Thom. "13 Issues for Churches in 2013." *ChurchLeaders*, January 15, 2013. https://tinyurl.com/y54o8gyu.

Reno, R. R. "Catholicism after 2018." *First Things*, October 2018. https://tinyurl.com/ybptjz8t.

Robert, Dana. *Christian Mission: How Christianity Became a World Religion.* Malden, MA: Wiley-Blackwell, 2009.

Rutledge, Fleming. *The Crucifixion: Understanding the Death of Jesus Christ.* Grand Rapids: Eerdmans, 2015.

Sayer, George. *Jack: A Life of C. S. Lewis.* Wheaton, IL: Crossway, 1988.

Scherer, Paul. *The Word God Sent.* New York: Harper and Row, 1965.

Schoon, Christopher James. *Cultivating an Evangelistic Character: Integrating Worship and Discipleship in the Missional Church.* Eugene, OR: Wipf and Stock, 2018.

Schumacher, E. F. *Small Is Beautiful: Economics as If People Mattered.* London: Blond and Briggs, 1973.

Siegele-Wenschkewitz, Leonore. "Christians against Nazis: The German Confessing Church." *Christianity Today.* Accessed December 4, 2020. https://tinyurl.com/y5ubwxnj.

Snyder, Anne. "Wrestling with Loyalty in a Fractured Age." *Comment*, January 2, 2020, 4–7.

Sparks, Paul, Tim Soerens, and Dwight J. Friesen. *The New Parish: How Neighborhood Churches Are Transforming Mission, Discipleship and Community.* Downers Grove, IL: InterVarsity, 2014.

Stackhouse, Reginald. "Church Planting in the 1950s: A Historical Perspective." In *Green Shoots out of Dry Ground*, edited by John P. Bowen, 35–42. Portland, OR: Wipf and Stock, 2013.

Stafford, Tim. "Go and Plant Churches of All Peoples: Crusades and Personal Witnessing Are No Longer the Cutting Edge of Evangelism." *Christianity Today*, September 27, 2007. https://tinyurl.com/34vfrh.

——. "Historian Ahead of His Time." *Christianity Today*, February 8, 2007, https://tinyurl.com/y5qbo8vr.

Stark, Rodney. *The Rise of Christianity: How the Obscure, Marginal Jesus Movement Became the Dominant Religious Force in the Western World in a Few Centuries*. New York: HarperCollins, 1996.

Stetzer, Ed. "Call Yourself a Christian? Start Talking about Jesus Christ." *Washington Post*, May 19, 2016. https://tinyurl.com/y4c8rktk.

Stott, John R. W. *Basic Christianity*. 1958. Reprint, London: InterVarsity, 1974.

——. *Christian Mission in the Modern World*. Downers Grove, IL: InterVarsity, 1975.

——. *Evangelical Theology: A Personal Plea for Unity*. Leicester: InterVarsity, 1999.

——. *God's New Society: The Message of Ephesians*. Downers Grove, IL: InterVarsity, 1979.

——. *The Radical Disciple: Some Neglected Aspects of Our Calling*. Downers Grove, IL: InterVarsity, 2009.

Taylor, John V. *The Go-Between God: The Holy Spirit and the Christian Mission*. London: SCM, 1972.

Tickle, Phyllis. *The Great Emergence: How Christianity Is Changing and Why*. Grand Rapids: Baker, 2008.

Tolkien, J. R. R. *The Lord of the Rings*. London: HarperCollins, 2004.

Tyson, John R. *The Way of the Wesleys: A Short Introduction*. Grand Rapids: Eerdmans, 2014.

Vonnegut, Kurt, Jr. "Who Am I This Time?" In *Welcome to the Monkey House*, 14–26. New York: Dell, 1950.

Wake, Andrew. *The Good Enough Parent: How to Provide for Your Child's Social and Emotional Development*. Bayswater, Victoria, Australia: Palmer Higgs, 2012.

Walking the Good Road: The Gospel and Acts with Ephesians—First Nations Version. N.p.: Great Thunder, 2017.

Walls, Andrew. *The Missionary Movement in Christian History: Studies in the Transmission of Faith*. Maryknoll, NY: Orbis, 1996.

Willard, Dallas. *The Divine Conspiracy: Rediscovering Our Hidden Life in God*. San Francisco: HarperCollins, 1997.

——. *Knowing Christ Today: Why We Can Trust Spiritual Knowledge*. New York: HarperCollins, 2009. Kindle.

Williams, Rowan. Lecture at "Changing the Landscape: Making the Mixed Economy Work." Oxford, UK. May 6, 2011. tinyurl.com/1052l0g5.

——. *Luminaries: Twenty Lives That Illuminate the Christian Way*. London: SPCK, 2019.

Willimon, William H. *The Intrusive Word: Preaching to the Unbaptized.* Grand Rapids: Eerdmans, 1994.

Winsa, Patty. "Sale of Local Church Brings a Chance for Reinvention." *Toronto Star*, December 5, 2010. https://tinyurl.com/y6ftrn8c.

Wright, Christopher. *The Mission of God: Unlocking the Bible's Grand Narrative.* Downers Grove, IL: InterVarsity, 2006.

Wright, N. T. *The Challenge of Jesus: Rediscovering Who Jesus Was and Is.* Downers Grove, IL: InterVarsity, 2015.

——. *The New Testament and the People of God.* Minneapolis: Fortress, 1992.

——. *Thinking in a New Way: How Paul Invented "Christian Theology."* E-book from a lecture at Duke Divinity School, Durham, NC, November 2014. https://ntwrightonline.org/paul-bonus-content.

Yoder, John Howard. *The Fullness of Christ: Paul's Vision of Universal Ministry.* Elgin, IL: Brethren, 1987.